## 2001:
### ON THE EDGE OF ETERNITY

Dr.
Jack
Van
Impe

# 2001:

## ON THE EDGE OF ETERNITY

*A biblical perspective
on what to expect in
the next millennium,
when to anticipate it,
and how to prepare for
Christ's earthly reign.*

WORD PUBLISHING

Dallas•London•Vancouver•Melbourne

2001: On the Edge of Eternity

Scriptures quoted were taken from the King James Version of the Bible (KJV).

The material contained in this book is based on data gathered by a team of researchers, and represents the most up-to-date information available at press time.

**Library of Congress Cataloging-in-Publication Data**
Van Impe, Jack.
    2001 : on the edge of eternity / Jack Van Impe.
      p.  cm.
    Includes bibliographical references.
    ISBN 0-8499-3891-0
    1. Bible—Prophecies—End of the world.   2. End of the world—
Biblical teaching.   3. Twenty-first century—Forecasts.
    4. Millennialism.    I. Title.
BS649.E63V26   1996
236'.9—dc20

        96-42158
        CIP

*Printed in the United States of America.*
6 7 8 0 1 2 3 4 9  QKP  9 8 7 6 5 4 3 2 1

*I dedicate this work to my wife and sweetheart, Rexella, who has faithfully ministered as vocal soloist in 1,100 city-wide crusades to over ten million people. Her interviews of more than 150 world leaders have been broadcast on national television and today she co-anchors our international telecasts.*

*My prayer is that we shall be alive and serving our Saviour together as we approach the glorious morning of Christ's return.*

# CONTENTS

## FOREWORD

I CAN THINK OF NO better way to begin this book than by thanking—and quoting—one of the most brilliant, thoughtful Christian writers of our day, my friend Dr. John F. Walvoord. This theologian, author, and man of God wrote in his landmark book, *The Millennial Kingdom:*

"The apostle Paul, in expressing the biblical hope of resurrection, delivered the dramatic pronouncement: 'If we have only hoped in Christ in this life we are of all men most pitiable' (1 Corinthians 15:19). What is true of the hope of resurrection is true of Christian hope in general. Faith without hope is just as dead as faith without works.

"The study of prophecy embracing as it does the totality of God's purpose and plan as revealed in the Scriptures is therefore neither trivial nor unimportant but the vital heart of all that is included in Christian faith. Though it is to be expected that the interpretation of prophecy should encounter difficulties, it is nevertheless the supreme goal of Biblical theology to determine what is the ordered and detailed program of future events prophesied in the Word of God."

This book is about the end times, the third millennium, the year 2001 and beyond. It describes our rapidly accelerating move toward the edge of eternity, and the events that are leading up to the glorious return of Jesus Christ to earth. As you read the first few chapters, you may say, "Dr. Van Impe, this is enlightening but shocking. You talk about a worldwide epidemic of AIDS, more and more frequent earthquakes, a proliferation of riots, crime waves, plagues, pestilence, and worldwide pollution. These make the difficulties of the children of Israel seem mild in comparison."

Yes, I would have to agree that the subject matter of the last few chapters may be startling. But it's all true. I have not made up the facts, fudged on their interpretation, nor have I exaggerated the iniquitous condition of mankind as we know it today.

But chapters 1 through 9 are simply prologue to chapter 10, which speaks with joy and praise of what the present-day events are leading to. However, please don't read chapter 10 first. That would be like figuring out prematurely "who dunnit," thus removing the suspense of the story. I urge you to work through the chronology of these events. See them in the perspective of your own life. Then, when we raise the trumpets and shout our hallelujahs at the triumphal return of Christ, you will have seen what we had to go through to get to that final victory.

Second Timothy 3:13–17 reminds us in the last days,

"Evil men and seducers shall wax worse and worse, deceiving, and being deceived. But continue thou in the things which thou hast learned and hast been assured of, knowing of whom thou hast learned *them;*

And that from a child thou hast known the holy Scriptures, which are able to make thee wise unto salvation through faith which is in Christ Jesus.

All Scripture is given by inspiration of God, and *is* profitable for doctrine, for reproof, for correction, for instruction in righteousness: That the man of God may be perfect, thoroughly furnished unto all good works."

*—Dr. Jack Van Impe*
*Troy, Michigan*

## IT'S THE STUNNING TRUTH

THE YEARS 1999, 2000, 2001: everyone is talking about them. The Internet with its millions of daily users has "chat rooms" where the dawn of a new century is the focus of discussion. Organizations worldwide are building global strategies around the Web, and it is the favorite subject of marketing gurus. The year 2000 and beyond arouses widespread fear, speculation, excitement, terror, and bewilderment in the hearts of people everywhere. Advertisers are taking advantage of the theme to sell their widgets. It is fast becoming the centerpiece for the speeches of pundits, statesmen, and politicians. Economists, scientists, military leaders, social critics, environmentalists, and religious leaders refer to it at every opportunity.

Some tell us not to worry, that 2000 and beyond are just another set of uneventful years on a busy calendar. Not so, say others, who predict that the events to follow entry into the third millennium will re-shape our personal lives and disrupt our collective destinies for generations to come. One thing is certain: The advent of the twenty-first century has captivated the attention of virtually everyone.

You've seen the headlines:

READY OR NOT, HERE IT COMES

BEYOND THE YEAR 2000

HOW SAFE WILL THE WORLD BE?

SCENARIOS FOR THE NEXT 200 YEARS

THE NUCLEAR FAMILY GOES BOOM!

POSSIBILITIES FOR CATASTROPHE

KINGDOMS TO COME

TOO MANY PEOPLE

Why all the fuss? Why are so many people perched on their electronic soap boxes, telling us the world following A.D. 2000 will hold such intriguing, fascinating, and challenging prospects for mankind? Why might the first decade of the millennium be the most important ten years of our world? Are ancient predictions of a catastrophic end to the world as we know it about to come true? Are we *really* speeding headlong toward the end of time?

## TECHNOLOGICAL BREAKTHROUGHS

INNOVATIVE TECHNOLOGICAL changes are happening so fast that they make this morning's headlines obsolete by the 10 P.M. news. Vast social, political, and economic upheavals are transforming entire cultures. Breathtaking, breakneck development of mass communications, and the less dramatic but equally upending processes of urbanization and modernization are creating even more social uncertainties. What does all this mean to you and me, especially as we move toward the year 2000?

In 1932 Aldous Huxley took a frightening peek at the future in his prophetic work of fiction, *Brave New World,* in wnich he suggested a society that had deteriorated into little more than a drug culture. He described people so intimidated at the idea of intimacy that it was actually outlawed, replaced by humanity propagated via test-tube births. Was Huxley simply a few years off? Are we only now poised on the cusp of a non-fictional brave new world?

In his landmark book, *Third Wave*, Alvin Tofler asks,

> "Should we breed people with cowlike stomachs so they can digest grass and hay—thereby alleviating the food problems by modifying us to eat lower on the food chain? Should we biologically alter workers to fit job requirements—for example, creating pilots with faster reaction times or assembly-line workers neurologically designed to do our monotonous work for us?"

These are just some of the questions being asked by a new breed of informed, interneted scientists, philosophers, and laypersons These innovators have made personal commitments never to remain content with the status quo, but instead avow to push biological ethics, global financial restructuring, and human engineering beyond the horizon of current human understanding.

## INFORMATION OVERLOAD

AND THAT BRINGS us back to the extraordinary flow of information that levitates in cyberspace, awaiting travelers who sit at a computer terminal, hit a few keystrokes, and are instantly connected with the world through the Web. A recent Nielsen survey concluded that an astonishing twenty-four million Americans and Canadians aged sixteen and above had used the Internet during the three months prior to the study. To the delight of global marketers, a surprising two-and-a-half million Web users have purchased products or services over the Internet, with no end in sight to the cyberbuying frenzy. What does this new social and economic toy mean for the future? When will information overload be too much?

## POLITICAL TURMOIL

POLITICALLY, THE YEAR 2001 may well usher in a kind of international chaos unlike any we've never seen in our time. Recent threats from the Kremlin indicate that Russia the Bear is anything but in hibernation. Moscow media report that Russia's army has espoused a doctrine that calls for an invasion of Estonia, Latvia, and Lithuania, should these former Soviet States ever achieve their heartfelt desire of joining NATO. So much for lasting peace on that front! And always-in-the-news Israel continues to be buffeted by her nearby foes. That tiny piece of ancient real estate must now further contend with warheads based in southern Russian provinces aimed at her land and her people.

## NEW NATURAL DISCOVERIES

NATURAL PHENOMENA never before seen by mankind continue to make headlines. Recent reports told how the Hubble telescope continues to capture stunning new star formations. The *Los Angeles Times* rhapsodized that ". . . the gaseous towers, six trillion miles long, resemble stalagmites rising from a cavern floor, or the heads of sea serpents. At their edges can be seen finger-like protrusions, each with tips larger than our solar system, in which stars are embedded."

Comet Shoemaker-Levy 9's impact on Jupiter grabbed the attention of the entire world. Was it a sign? Enormous explosions, hundreds of times more powerful than all the earth's nuclear warheads, made people realize just how vulnerable our planet is to a similar occurrence. What is happening out there in our universe, in our own solar system, on our planet, and to our individual lives? Is something spectacular taking place before our eyes to which we should give greater heed than we have in the past? Are there hints in the heavens that are crying out for interpretation?

In Israel, Orthodox Jews took note that the crashes of Shoemaker-Levy 9 began on July 16, 1994, the eve of Tisha Be'av, the traditional day of mourning for disasters that have struck the Jewish people throughout their history. Comets, the *Jerusalem Report* pointed out, have long been seen as harbingers of doom—by Jews and non-Jews alike. The rabbis of the Lubavitch movement believe that the Jupiter bombardment signals the return of their Messiah as described in the Zohar and Talmud.

## EARTHQUAKES, PLAGUES, AND FAMINE

THERE'S ALSO a whole lot of shaking going on. A recent *Deutsche Press Agentur* report provided this astonishing news: Earthquakes have killed two million people so far this century, and about half of those have died in natural catastrophes. The toll keeps rising with recent killer quakes striking Chile, Bolivia, Colombia, and Indonesia.

A PLAGUE ON ALL YOUR HOUSES could be the headline for most of our world's newspapers, as more than thirty new strains of the AIDS virus threaten to ravage the earth's population. Meanwhile, vying for top-billing on the list of horrors, in 1994 people were terrorized by the spread of Strep-A, the dreaded flesh-eating infection. These new plagues have emerged at a time when antibiotics, the great hope of the twentieth century, have begun to lose their effectiveness. Today's diseases mutate, exchange drug-resistant genes with one another, and evolve faster than pharmaceutical companies can invent new treatments.

> Today's diseases mutate ... faster than pharmaceutical companies can invent new treatments.

"Let them eat cake," the saying goes. But more than likely the poor will have to eat leaves and insects, or in many cases, nothing at all. More than twenty-six million men, women, and children are facing starvation in East Africa alone: Drought, war, malaria, and hunger are afflicting the populations in Sudan, Uganda, Rwanda, Burundi, Tanzania, Eritrea, Ethiopia, Djibouti, Somalia, and Kenya.

And all this is only the tip of the apocalyptic iceberg, because there's more to come. Keep reading the papers—but read with understanding. Keep watching the news—but view the reports with discernment. Look for the signs, wherever they may be, because they will be clues to the future of the world and its leadership. Take, for example, the remarks of a former NATO official who said, "What we want is a man of sufficient stature to hold the allegiances of all people and to lift us out of the economic morass into which we are sinking. Send us such a man, and be he god or devil, we will receive him."

In man's search for international leadership, there has always been the drive to find the one who is destined to hold it all together. Are people today really ready to accept a "devil" as the new CEO of world affairs? Could this NATO official have been speaking prophetically of events to come center-stage in the year 1999 and beyond? The signs are all around us, and he who has eyes to see, let him see.

## A SCIENTIST'S BELIEF

OVER THE PAST several months I have poured over encyclopedias, shelves of books on church history, more than fifty secular historical analyses of our civilization, and a multitude of religious treatises that speak to the issues of the year 2000 and beyond. In my research I was particularly moved by a comment made by the great scientist Sir Isaac Newton, by all counts one of the most formidable thinkers in the history of our world and a towering figure in the scientific revolution of the seventeenth century. Newton said, "About the time of the end, a body of men will be raised up who will turn their attention to the prophecies and insist upon their literal interpretation in the midst of much clamor and opposition."

Newton's words are especially fascinating because in his day people still regarded the world as square—the kind of flat, frightening planet where sea captains, their ships and precious cargo were forever in danger of falling into the great abyss where dragons lurked to devour and destroy all unsuspecting prey.

A Christian believer, Newton recognized that the "four corners of the earth" referred to in Scripture were simply the four directions of the compass—north, south, east, and west. Further, as a scientist, Newton saw no contradictions whatsoever between the Bible and scientific speculation of his day. The great scholar and thinker was well aware of the meaning of Isaiah 40:22. . . . *"It is* he that sitteth upon the circle of the earth, and the inhabitants thereof *are* as grasshoppers; that stretcheth out the heavens as a curtain, and spreadeth them out as a tent to dwell in."

I wonder what a poll of Newton's townsfolk would have revealed about their view on religion, the Bible, and the direction of their world. What would they have said about the future and what it held for them? We'll never know with any certainty. We do know something about today's citizens, however—about where they are now, and where they imagine they and their families are headed by the year 2000.

## THE POLL ASKS: WHAT ABOUT THE MILLENNIUM?

REPORTING IN a special edition of *Time* Magazine in the fall of 1992, a *Time*/CNN telephone poll posed several intriguing questions to eight hundred adult Americans, asking them what they thought life would be like in the next millennium. The pollster's questions solicited candid opinions on the future of American society, status of religion, importance of communications, comparison of present and past political leadership, and perceived future global political and economic threats.

Here are some of those questions and responses by percentage:

Q: COMPARED WITH THE TWENTIETH CENTURY, DO YOU THINK THE
TWENTY-FIRST CENTURY WILL HAVE MORE:

> *Wars: 32 percent*
>
> *Environmental disasters: 59 percent*
>
> *Poverty: 61 percent*
>
> *Disease: 53 percent*
>
> *Hope for the future: 62 percent*

Q: DO YOU THINK THE WORLD WILL BE IN BETTER SHAPE AT THE
END OF THE TWENTY-FIRST CENTURY THAN IT IS TODAY?

> *Better: 41 percent*
>
> *Worse: 32 percent*
>
> *About the same: 15 percent*

Q. WHICH COUNTRY WILL BE THE GREATEST THREAT TO THE U.S.'S
DOMINANT POSITION IN WORLD AFFAIRS IN THE TWENTY-FIRST
CENTURY?

> *Germany: 7 percent*
>
> *Iraq: 7 percent*
>
> *China: 13 percent*
>
> *Russia: 14 percent*
>
> *Japan 22 percent*

Q: WILL RELIGION PLAY A GREATER ROLE IN THE LIVES OF PEOPLE
IN THIS COUNTRY AFTER THE YEAR 2000?

> *Greater: 55 percent*
>
> *Lesser: 27 percent*

Q: WILL THE SECOND COMING OF JESUS CHRIST OCCUR SOMETIME
IN THE NEXT THOUSAND YEARS?

> *Yes: 53 percent*
>
> *No: 31 percent*

Will humans make regular trips to other planets? Will a woman be president of the U.S.? Will scientists find a remedy for the common cold? Will there be a cure for AIDS? Even if you did not receive a call from *Time*/CNN, what would your answers have been? What do you think the next millennium will hold for you, your family, your church, your country?

One thing is certain—we are a nation of armchair quarterbacks with millions of opinions. Some have suggested the next thousand years will represent the death and rebirth of mankind's former attempts to make civilization work. Others see the millennium as one last chance to chase our dreams and aspirations, a final attempt to learn from history, a brief window of opportunity to put our houses in order and to engage in a kind of cosmic sleight-of-hand that somehow will make things right once and for all.

> What will the next millennium hold for you?

In the midst of this speculation, however, there are key questions that seldom enter the public forum at large. What does God's Word have to say about the future of our world? What does the Bible tell us to expect, from whom, and when? What can you and I specifically hope to see God do on earth as we approach the year 2000 and the years beyond?

Because so few seem to be asking these critical questions as we move closer to the millennium's threshold, I felt it necessary to write this book, *2001: On the Edge of Eternity*. In fact, it may be the most important book I've ever written, and it is my earnest prayer that the pages to follow will put this historic era into a thoughtful biblical perspective.

Consider this word from Isaiah, chapter 28, verses 9 and 10:

> "Whom shall he teach knowledge? and whom shall he make to understand doctrine? *them that are* weaned from the milk, and drawn from the breasts. For precept *must be* upon precept, precept upon precept; line upon line, line upon line; here a little, *and* there a little. . . ."

God must have wanted us to pay particular attention to those verses or he would not have repeated Himself: precept must be upon precept, *precept upon precept;* line upon line, *line upon line.* It is common for pastors and Bible teachers to engage in expository preaching where they review each sentence of God's Word and interpret it precept by precept, line by line. Why should we not pursue that same line of reasoning as it relates to understanding prophecy and to what God says about earth's final days?

In 2 Timothy 3:1 the apostle Paul reminds us, "This know also, that in the last days perilous times shall come." Paul then goes on to speak of the devastating, dehumanizing behavior that will be key ingredients in those end times—when men shall be lovers of their own selves, covetous, boasters, proud,

> "This know also, that in the last days perilous times shall come."
> —2 Timothy 3:1

blasphemers, disobedient to parents. This sounds painfully like the evening news and reads like the headlines of countless city newspapers. So what is the problem in taking this passage of God's Word literally? A person would have to be living under a rock not to see the truth and understand the implications of what was written centuries ago. But we shouldn't believe in prophetic writings simply because we're seeing them fulfilled on CNN or on nightly news broadcasts. We should accept their reality for an even better reason: God has communicated these truths to us in His Word.

## CHAOTIC WEATHER CONDITIONS

ARE THESE, IN FACT, perilous times? Just how perilous are they? We've already cited several current events in this chapter, and to the list of doom-and-gloom we can add increasingly strange, new weather patterns which are playing havoc with our world. The Worldwatch Institute recently reported that carbon emissions, deforestation, and soil erosion are worsening. Birds are disappearing. Destructive insects are developing resistance to pesticides. The seas are producing fewer harvests of edible fish. Grain stocks are down. Tropical rain forests are dwindling. This is not a pretty sight, nor will the picture become much brighter in the days ahead. In fact, the chaos has just begun, as we will learn in later chapters.

## THE PLAGUE OF RELIGIOUS DECEPTION

IT'S BAD ENOUGH to observe the blatant disregard for the condition of our physical world, but even more perilous is the continued religious deception plaguing the planet and the countries abroad. Humanism, the corrupt notion that man is at the center of the universe, has become the religion promoted in schools, the media, and throughout the allegedly "enlightened" Western world. Meanwhile, militant Islam is on the march throughout the Middle East and Central Asia, with more than one billion adherents worldwide.

In fact, Islam is growing faster than Christianity for the first time in world history. In the meantime, teachings of non-monotheistic Eastern religions have infected even the church itself, driving it increasingly toward apostasy and a laissez faire interpretation of God's Word. With widespread religious deception so out of control, it is easy to understand how worldwide ecclesiastical trends are leading to the dawn of a one-world church controlled by the spirits of Satan.

Notice the words of the last book of the New Testament, Revelation 9:21, "Neither repented they of their murders, nor of their sorceries, nor of their fornication, nor of their thefts." This passage in Revelation refers to the tribulation hour and the judgments that will descend on mankind because of blatant sins committed by humanity. Then, in the midst of this fiery judgment from above, we learn there will be no expression of remorse, no repentance, no sense of seeking forgiveness for murder, drug abuse, fornication, sexual promiscuity, or theft. These are being played out on television screens and in news magazines every day.

## GOOD-BYE, SWEET SUBURBS

MINDLESS GANG WARFARE now takes place in the streets of our inner cities and once-quiet suburbs. Drive-by shootings steal the lives of innocent children caught in the crossfire. Murderers kill for kicks, and sociopathic monsters walk the streets searching for yet more prey. Total disregard for the lives of the unborn corrupts huge segments of society. It is difficult to determine whether our quality of life is getting better or worse. Are our lives becoming more secure with each techno-logical advance, or is our society coming apart at the seams? Perhaps all this has something to do with the end of time, and with events that will occur during the millennium.

## THE DRY BONES ARE FOR REAL!

WHILE THERE ARE certainly portions of Scripture to be treated symbolically, there are many more that must be interpreted literally. For example, in Ezekiel chapter 37. We read the well-known story about the prophet's vision in the valley of the dry bones. We learn how at the end of history these bones will arise from their graveyards. As they make their appear-ance in a later age, suddenly sinew and flesh will begin to form on these decaying bones. What was dead will live again. What was once useless and inert will come back into exis-tence with great force and vitality. "Oh, that's just figurative language and a parable," some will say. "Impossible! That's not a real future event. Only symbolic," other commentators will insist.

But I say, "No, No, No!" It cannot be symbolic, because in the same chapter, verse 11, God gives the precise interpreta-tion of the story. His Word says, "Then he said unto me, Son of man, these bones are the whole house of Israel: behold, they say, Our bones are dried, and our hope is lost: we are cut off for our parts."

What is literally supposed to happen to these bones? They are destined to come back from the nations and return to their own land. This is not figurative language. It is not a parable. It is literal and, in fact, it has already happened. Let's go back to Ezekiel 36:24 where we learn, "For I will take you from among the heathen, and gather you out of all countries, and will bring you into your own land." Why struggle for a figurative meaning when God's Holy Word is meant to be taken at face value? Dry bones did, in fact, come to life. God forever honors His promises.

God is speaking to His Jewish people—gathering them out of all nations and bringing them back to their own land. The Jews were literally buried in the nations of the world—their graveyards—in Gentile countries where they were oppressed, suppressed, and distressed beyond measure. But all that would change, promised Ezekiel, and it did change. God honored His promise and brought His people back from death—from a deserted, seemingly forgotten pile of dry, decaying bones—to their own home.

It happened on May 17, 1948 when the new Israel ran up a six-pointed star of David on a flagpole in Jerusalem. Dry bones received life. Sinew once again adhered to bones once thought to be lifeless and without hope. This passage should persuade us that the Word of God has the answers we seek to understand our past, our present, and our future—literal answers for literal questions.

## Millennia One and Two

I've received letters recently from people who remind me that many things prophesied for the year 1000—the turn of the last millennium—never actually happened. Therefore, how can we predict with any accuracy what is to transpire in the next millennium? I have appreciated their letters and strong interest in this subject. Let me refer to an article written by David Crumb, who describes in some detail the spirit of the people on the eve of the end of that first millennium. The time is midnight, the last day of the year A.D. 999. Here is what Crumb says:

> "The last time the world faced the dawn of a millennium, thousands of people were in panic, convinced the planet would be dissolved into ashes at midnight on the last day of 999. Others were certain New Year's Day 1000 would see the Second Coming of Christ. Pope Sylvester stood motionless, arms upraised as he concluded mass at exactly midnight to end 999. As church bells tolled the fateful hour, the multitudes stood for a moment transfixed, but in the twinkling of an eye, were swept away in a frenzy of universal joy. Humanity had been given a new lease on life upon the earth that had been reborn. The year of fear and trembling had passed."

Whew! A collective sigh of relief. Others have noted that in the decade before the year A.D. 1000, men with shaggy hair swarmed across the face of Europe prophesying an imminent apocalypse, shouting, pleading, "The end is near! The end is near!" But the end was not near; nor did it ever come.

## THE YEAR A.D. 1000 REVISITED?

NOW, AS WE APPROACH the second millennium, there is similar hysteria building in the hearts and minds of many people. This time, however, it is not wild-eyed men with shaggy hair wandering from village to village who bring news of imminent demise. This time there is a message of doom from professionals, historians, educators, politicians, economists, and even military planners. Nonetheless, this takes us back to the original question: If people were so wrong about what should have transpired in the year 1000, why should we believe their descendants one thousand years later who dogmatically declare what will take place in the year 2000?

Good question. Let's look at it together. From the year 500 forward, there was a time in history known as the Dark Ages. Although modern historians tend to avoid using the term because of its value-laden implications of barbarism and intellectual darkness, the phrase "Dark Ages" was appropriate.

This desolate era of cultural stagnation and regression was sandwiched between the glory of classical antiquity and the rebirth of that glory in the beginnings of the modern world. There was little cultural stimulation. Intellectual thought had come to a standstill. There was virtually no wisdom literature. There were no printed Bibles, so there was no knowledge of biblical prophecy or awareness of the end times. Consequently, there was no cogent thinking about what could possibly happen at the end of the first millennium. The people of this period really were in the dark—intellectually, socially, and spiritually. How could they know the times that lay ahead in the next millennium?

Second Peter 1:19 reminds us, "We have also a more sure word of prophecy; whereunto ye do well that ye take heed, as unto a light that shineth in a dark place, until the day dawn, and the day star arise in your hearts."

Why do we have this assurance? Because of what we read two verses later in 2 Peter 1:21: "For the prophecy came not in old time by the will of man: but holy men of God spake *as they were* moved by the Holy Ghost."

If only the people in the Dark Ages could have read the following scriptures, and had been aware of the "six-day theory," based on them:

"For a thousand years in thy sight *are but* as yesterday when it is past, and *as* a watch in the night."

—PSALM 90:4

"But, beloved, be not ignorant of this one thing, that one day *is* with the Lord as a thousand years, and a thousand years as one day."

—2 PETER 3:8

Because God created the world in six days, the "six-day theory" holds that the world will go on for six thousand years. From Adam to Christ, four thousand years passed—or four days. From Christ until the year 1000 was another day, amounting to five days: four days from the Old Testament, and one from the New Testament era. Had they had access to these biblical references, the prophets of doom at the close of the first century would have known that the earth wasn't about to end after all. The "sixth day" would not conclude until the year 2000, and perhaps as far ahead as the year 2012, as we'll note in later chapters.

**What is the "six-day theory"?**

## THE MILLENNIUM AND CHILIASM

TO HAVE A THOROUGH understanding of the word *millennium,* let's look at the original language derivatives for this word. In Latin, *mille* means "thousand"; *annus* means "years." The Greeks also had a term for this which they called *chilias*—meaning "one thousand." In this book, whenever we use the terms *millennial, millennialism,* or *chiliasm,* the meaning is always "a thousand years."

This is important historically because most of the great church fathers taught that anyone who did not believe in chiliasm—the literal one-thousand-year reign of Christ on earth—was a heretic. Some still believe that when Christ comes to earth it will signal the end of the world. If this is your theological point of view, it may come as a surprise to you to hear quotes to the contrary from some of the greatest scholars, Rabbis, and church fathers of church history.

For example, a man by the name of Delitich had this to say about the early church and its millennial teachings:

"Chiliasm was the faith of the early church. Irenaeus the Great—like Justin, the most learned man of his time—categorized and held as promoters of heresy and even of blasphemy all those who denied the chiliastic faith which, in their day, was the test of an orthodox church. In other words, if you didn't believe that, you were an unbeliever."

The reign of Christ on earth will be for a thousand years. Not to believe this is to be out of sync with the earliest of Christian writings. The truth of this belief remains irrefutable.

These are the words of the early church fathers, the leaders during the first three hundred years of Christianity. If, in their day, you did not believe in chiliasm—the reign of Christ on earth for a thousand years—you were considered a heretic. Therefore, those in modern times who teach this biblical truth are not heretics, as some would perhaps believe. On the contrary. We are simply espousing the teachings of some of the greatest church fathers in ecclesiastical history—men such as Bishop Hippolytus, Irenaeus, Tertullian, Justin Martyr, and a number of others.

> The faith of the early church of Jesus Christ was chiliastic. . . .

There is another more recent historian, Dr. Nathaniel West, who speaks about chiliasm. He says, "Such is the Jewish origin of our Christian faith, the faith of the early Jewish Christian church, the faith of the pre-Christian rabbis, the faith of God's people under the old covenant, the faith of the prophets, a chiliastic faith and a chiliastic kingdom of glory on earth. The vestibule and prelude to eternal blessedness."

This is the premise of this book. And from this premise, we offer substantial proof of the events most likely to occur during the next millennium—our countdown to eternity. Why is this fulcrum of faith so vital as we stand at the door of the next thousand years? Because the faith of the early church of Jesus Christ was chiliastic—holding fast to the belief that there would literally be a thousand-year reign of Christ. It is irrefutable. It cannot be argued against with any seriousness. Yet, for hundreds of years many believers were confused and thrown off base by some of the statements made by the brilliant fifth-century Christian leader, Augustine.

Augustine held his ground when he said that whenever the word "Israel" is mentioned in the Scriptures, it means "church." And when the Bible talks about "Israel going home to its own special land," he maintained that this really refers to a "Christian going home to God in heaven."

As I ponder the other significant writings of this man of God, it becomes even more difficult for me to understand how a scholar as brilliant as Augustine could concoct such an erroneous, nonsensical interpretation of God's Word. It simply cannot be interpreted in that light without doing serious damage to other relevant Scripture.

Isaiah 2:3 reminds us, "And many people shall go and say, Come ye, and let us go up to the mountain of the LORD, to the house of the God of Jacob; and he will teach us of his ways, and we will walk in his paths: for out of Zion shall go forth the law, and the word of the LORD from Jerusalem."

This passage must be taken literally. It is when the law is being administered out of Jerusalem as Messiah comes that they beat their swords into plowshares and their spears into pruning hooks—the subject of the next verse. But who is in charge? Again, the prophet Isaiah in chapter 9, verse 6 gives us one of the most beautiful themes in all of Scripture,

"For unto us a child is born, unto us a son is given:"

(That's when He returns.)

"and the government shall be upon his shoulder:"

(The government has never been on Christ's shoulders, but it is coming.)

Then when we come to Micah 4:3, we read the text again,

> "And he shall judge among many people, and rebuke strong nations afar off; and they shall beat their swords into plowshares, and their spears into pruning hooks: nation shall not lift up a sword against nation, neither shall they learn war any more."

The world today is attempting to engage in this Herculean peacemaking effort without *Moshiach*—without Christ. And it isn't working. But what peace there will be when this great event actually takes place—peace that truly passes all understanding! This will be a global time of healing as *Moshiach,* the Great Physician, is with us, ushering in an even more blessed day, described so graphically in Isaiah 35:5–6

> **This will be a global time of healing . . .**

> "Then the eyes of the blind shall be opened, and the ears of the deaf shall be unstopped. Then shall the lame man leap as a hart, and the tongue of the dumb sing: for in the wilderness shall waters break out, and streams in the desert."

This event will, and must, take place on planet earth. This is why it is so important that we stop spiritualizing the prophecies of God. Instead, let us take God at His Word—literally. He loves us literally. He saves us literally. And the prophecies of the end time are literally true, as we will continue to demonstrate in biblical context throughout the remainder of this book.

Meanwhile, the key questions remain: What will, in fact, take place during Christ's reign of one thousand years? How will this play into the events occurring in the year 2001? What will society look like during the second millennium? How will things be different for the believer? And what have the church fathers, the Rabbis, the Targum, Talmud,

Midrash, and other ancient Jewish writings said about this great millennial event? One thing is certain. These thousand years of our soon-to-come millennium are real, not imaginary. They are actual, not a mere ideal.

## WHAT THE RABBIS HAD TO SAY . . .

**A** FRIEND TOLD ME A STORY recently about an aerial photographer who worked for a well-known magazine. This professional had been assigned to shoot a raging forest fire in a remote area. His company had arranged for a single-engine plane to fly him over the fire for his picture-taking expedition.

He arrived at the small airstrip a few minutes before sundown. As he rolled onto the tarmac, the pilot of the Cessna was waiting. The photographer jumped in with his many bags of equipment and, over the drone of the engine, shouted, "Okay, let's go."

The young pilot moved the small craft into the wind and within moments they were in the air.

"I want you to fly over the northeast side of the fire," said the photographer, "make several passes, and get as low as you can."

With fear in his voice, the nervous pilot pleaded, "Why would we do that, sir?"

"Because I'm going to take pictures," said the photographer. "I'm a photographer, and photographers take pictures. That's why my magazine sent me to this area."

After a long pause, the cotton-mouthed pilot replied, "You mean, you're not the flight instructor?"

I can see the fear on the face of that young pilot now. He didn't get what he expected. He wanted help, not images on film. He wanted to know the way, not be put in harm's way. He thought he was in good hands, but in the end, his safety and the safety of his passenger were in his own hands.

I like that story because its message is crystal-clear. It makes a lot of difference where we get our information. It matters how we interpret the events that continue to assault our senses through television, radio, and the printed page.

In chapter 1 we set the stage for some of the human and physical trauma escalating unabated before our eyes: the pain of new plagues, worldwide earthquakes, changing weather patterns, unrelenting famine, and ongoing political unrest. But that was only the tip of the iceberg. For us to come to grips with what to expect as we approach the year 2000 and beyond, we must look through the headlines and beyond the sound bites to what is really happening as we approach the countdown to eternity. With that objective in mind, let's continue our litany of current events that remind us how fast time's earthly clock is ticking.

> We must look through the headlines and beyond the sound bites to what is really happening as we approach the countdown to eternity.

## THE CHALLENGES WITH WHICH WE LIVE

- Russia is moving ahead with its plans to build a one-billion-dollar nuclear plant in Iran—serious trouble for the free world.

- U.S. intelligence officials remain in the dark about the extent of the damage done by CIA turncoat-spy Aldrich Ames. Ames' wanton ransacking of several top-secret files led to the executions of at least ten military and intelligence officers secretly working for the United States within the old Soviet System. We may never know the ultimate implications of this treachery.

● Within minutes after you read this paragraph, the U.S. government debt will have sped light years past a five-trillion-dollar plateau—an astronomical figure that an array of experts fear may bankrupt the nation in one way or another. This is hardly a "welcome wagon" experience for the grandchildren of the future.

● A recent State Department report indicates that 40 percent of Mexico's economy is dependent on illegal drug trafficking to the United States. The selfishness and greed of a few are destroying the lives of our best and brightest here at home.

● Russia and Libya have signed a $1.5 billion deal on joint energy projects, including oil and gas pipelines, power stations, and electricity transmission lines. Woe to the naive who believe the Russian bear is in hibernation.

● Persian Gulf sheikdoms in Bahrain, Kuwait, Oman, Qatar, and the United Arab Emirates all feel the threat of a combination of internal discontent bred by Islamic fundamentalists, and the external military and missionary zeal of Iran. There is trouble among the Islamic brotherhood—with serious international mischief about to take place as never before.

### ISRAEL DOVES FEAR IRANIAN NUKES

SHIMON PERES, Israel's former Prime Minister, is known throughout international circles as an optimist. This man, considered most responsible for Jerusalem's gamble on peace talks with the Palestinians, was often criticized for placing too much emphasis on diplomacy, and not enough on military preparedness. Yet

Peres warned the world about what may be the greatest danger to peace since Adolph Hitler—the Islamic bomb.

Europe and the West, said Peres, are in danger of being held hostage by Islamic fundamentalists armed with nuclear weapons. He predicted that Iran—or some other Muslim nation—will acquire or develop a nuclear capability within the next four or five years.

"Time is running out," Peres stated bluntly. "The fundamentalists could take over the oil wells. They could play with the European economy like a toy. This could happen anywhere in the Gulf, and I include Saudi Arabia. It's not the first time we've faced an evil movement, but it's the first time in history an evil movement has had the chance to acquire nuclear weapons."

> **"Time is running out."**
> **—Shimon Peres**

I wonder if the Old Testament pages of former foreign minister Peres are dog-eared to selected portions of scripture, such as Psalm 83:4: "They have said, Come, and let us cut them off from *being* a nation; that the name of Israel may be no more in remembrance."

Or Malachi 4:1: "For, behold, the day cometh, that shall burn as an oven; and all the proud, yea, and all that do wickedly, shall be stubble: and the day that cometh shall burn them up, saith the LORD of hosts, that it shall leave them neither root nor branch."

Or Ezekiel 38:5: "Persia, Ethiopia, and Libya with them; all of them with shield and helmet."

As Mikhail Gorbachev has said, "What is emerging is a more complex global structure of international relations, an awareness of the need for some kind of global government—one in which all members of the world community would take part—is gaining ground."

Is this all a crazy, random coincidence? Were the prophets of old just enormously lucky to predict events that would come to pass generations after they walked the face of the earth? Are the reports of wars and rumors of wars that occupy much of the ink on our front pages simply interesting copy for a populace that feeds on violence and expressions of misconduct? Or is something profoundly dangerous really going on? Is the clock of time as we know it truly winding down? Are the events before us telling us something about the countdown to eternity to which we should pay greater heed? There is still more evidence of a confluence of events that will bring us inevitably closer to the end.

## PROGRESS OF EUROPEAN UNION

ACCORDING TO estimates by a British think tank, two Europeans in three will be participating in complete monetary union by 1999. In 1992 a U.S. cabinet member observed: "Within the next hundred years nationhood as we know it will be obsolete; all states will recognize a single global authority. . . .

"All countries are basically social arrangements. No matter how permanent and even sacred they may seem at any one time, in fact they are all artificial and temporary."

Early in 1995, United Nation officials proposed the creation of a global tax at the World Summit on Social Development in Copenhagen, Denmark. Several plans were floated, but the most frequently discussed option was the "Tobin Tax," a UN levy on foreign exchange transactions first proposed sixteen years ago by economist James Tobin.

The money would be gathered by national governments and pooled into an account controlled by the IMF—the International Monetary Fund. The money collected would be used to create new wealth transfer programs—a kind of international welfare system—as well as to finance UN "peace-keeping" missions around the world.

As you read the above comment, lay your Bible alongside it and open to Revelation 13, verses 7 and 17:

"And it was given unto him to make war with the saints, and

to overcome them: and power was given him over all kindreds, and tongues, and nations. . . . And that no man might buy or sell, save he that had the mark, or the name of the beast, or the number of his name."

This is all warp and woof of an intricate millennial fabric being woven before the eyes of all, and it has everything to do with 2001 and the edge of eternity. Yet, prone to deception, standing for nothing, and therefore destined to fall for anything, the spiritually naive continue to live in "La La Land," hoping for the best as they chase shadows of "truth" in their earnest desire for personal fulfillment. As C. S. Lewis reminds us, no assortment of bad eggs makes for a good omelet. Chasing the wind is a futile effort. Still, the chase continues.

## FALSE PROPHETS ARISE

JESUS WARNED his followers in Matthew 24:24. "For there shall arise false Christs, and false prophets, and shall show great signs and wonders; insomuch that, *if it were* possible, they shall deceive the very elect."

In the closing moments of this present age, just as World War III appears inevitable, a great leader will come to international prominence, proclaiming, "Peace, Peace!" He will jet from one nation to another negotiating his proposals. The world will say, "This is it! Utopia! Peace!"

How carefully do you read the morning and evening papers? How do you interpret the events covered by the ubiquitous eye of CNN? What is your impression of the news as it speeds over the Internet, through E-mail, via newsletters, and instant "this just in" reports from every media source possible? As the world approaches a new millennium, the stage is increasingly filled with dangerous apostates, coming from the wings to play their devious parts, seize their ethereal "fifteen minutes of fame," and take with them an audience of the gullible and uninformed to a place of confusion and delusion.

For most observers, the activities of these individuals appear to be no more than harmless shenanigans carried out by kooks, wizards of the bizarre, and charlatans. However, those who have eyes to see and ears to ear—people who know and

> ... A great leader will come to international prominence, proclaiming, "Peace, Peace!"

understand the times—recognize a far greater danger in their widespread international popularity. This is not a time to view their influence as business as usual. Never in our world's history have we seen such a plethora of wolves in sheep's clothing. Here's a brief sampling of current distractions:

- Shoko Asahara went through failed careers as an acupuncturist and health-tonic salesman before becoming the "venerated master" of the Aum Supreme Truth cult in Japan. He became the prime suspect in a deadly nerve gas attack that killed ten people and hospitalized thousands of Japanese train commuters. Asahara boasts that he's able to defy gravity, while his followers parade around Tokyo wearing elephant masks. He praises with equal enthusiasm Buddhist saints and Adolph Hitler, whom he lauds as a "true prophet."

- In California, the city of San Jose spent half-a-million dollars to build a twenty five-foot-high statue of Quetzalcoatl, an ancient Mayan god whose pagan cult condoned and practiced human sacrifice. Quetzalcoatl translates into English as "plumed serpent." The bronze statue depicts a coiled, feathered snake.

- The neo-pagan "goddess movement" is gaining momentum in the West, especially within mainline Christian denominations. Norma Turner, a former Roman Catholic nun, was introduced to "goddess spirituality" when she was thirty-six years old. Today, she worships full moons and harvest times. This neo-pagan movement now holds conventions throughout the United States—often in Christian churches.

I continually see news briefings, intelligence reports, and television commentaries all pointing to the same conclusion. But, for the moment, let's leave the temporary comments of the daily press, the guessing games of the pundits, and the television coverage to review what God's Word and the wisdom of the past have to say about where we've been, where we are now, and where we are headed.

## GOD'S TRUTH AND THE WISDOM OF THE AGES

THE QUESTION IS often asked: What have Jewish scholars traditionally believed about the end times? What did their writings reveal? How different—or how similar—have their conclusions been to those of Christian writers, thinkers, and historians? Did the learned rabbis of old, for example, believe in a literal millennium, or did they interpret those thousand years as mere interesting—and largely figurative—language? To help set the record straight, it is important to reflect on some of the rabbinical writings regarding this subject.

> The rabbis of antiquity believed in the coming of the Messiah.

The voice of the synagogue has always been opposed to any position that suggests the millennium is an unreliable figment of the imagination.

The Targum (Aramaic paraphrase of the Old Testament), Talmud (a vast compendium of Jewish law and lore), and Midrash (an interpretive method to penetrate the deepest meaning of a Hebrew passage) all have concluded there will be a literal thousand-year period when Messiah will reign on earth.

For example, Rabbi Keva wrote that the righteous Messiah will drink of the cup of life in the future age.

Rabbi Isaac recited Psalm 45 which speaks about King Messiah and His government of which there will be no end.

The rabbis of antiquity believed in the coming of Messiah, or Moshiach, the redeemer who is destined to come at an appointed time—during the millennium. This message of end-time hope and eternal promise continues to be taught in the religious curriculum of Jewish schools:

"We believe the Messiah will gather the dispersed of Israel, and restore the government to the house of David. We believe in the resurrection of the dead. We live in hope and expectation of the coming of Messiah, and our return to our fatherland, the land of Judah. The Psalms of Solomon pray imploringly for the gathering of the elect Israel, the establishment of the kingdom of mercy and kindness, Messiah's smiting of the earth with the word of his mouth forever, and the coming of a king to subdue the scepters or the rulers of all the earth."

What the rabbis have taught is also seen in biblical passages:

Revelation 19:16—"And he hath on his vesture and on his thigh a name written, KING OF KINGS, AND LORD OF LORDS."

Revelation 20:4—"And I saw thrones, and they sat upon them, and judgment was given unto them: and I *saw* the souls of them that were beheaded for the witness of Jesus, and for the word of God, and which had not worshipped the beast, neither his image, neither had received *his* mark upon their foreheads, or in their hands; and they lived and reigned with Christ a thousand years."

Psalm 2:6—"Yet have I set my king upon my holy hill of Zion."

Luke 1:32—"He shall be great, and shall be called the Son of the Highest: and the Lord God shall give unto him the throne of his father David."

Matthew 5:35—"Nor by the earth; for it is his footstool: neither by Jerusalem; for it is the city of the great King."

Zechariah 8:22—"Yea, many people and strong nations shall come to seek the LORD of hosts in Jerusalem, and to pray before the LORD."

Consider the following: If the Rabbis are talking about events to take place on or around the year 2000 A.D.—during the next millennium—then Elias, doctor of the second temple, makes a comment that is truly significant: "Messiah's kingdom is one thousand years, for the world's ages are distributed upon the type of the creative week." Jewish scholars generally agree that the world shall last six thousand years from its creation, or eighty-five jubilees from the time of Elias. Then the Son of David will come, and begin the world's rest (Sabattic rest).

## SIMPLE ARITHMETIC

AS WE NOTED in the last chapter, Jewish scholars arrive at this conclusion by interpreting Psalm 90, verse 4: "For a thousand years in thy sight are but as yesterday when it is past, and as a watch in the night." Since the Rabbis, and other traditional Jewish scholars, believed that God created the world in six one-thousand-year periods, they reasoned the world would continue for six thousand years. Simple arithmetic—and a careful calculation of the genealogical tables—shows that humanity "used up" four thousand years from Adam to Christ. This means there would be two days—or two thousand years—remaining to bring us to a complete six thousand years, which would culminate sometime around the year 2000. That would be the approximate time for Messiah's return. The Day of the Redeemed will have come, as they believed, in Isaiah 63:4 ". . . For the day of vengeance is in mine heart, and the year of my redeemed is come."

## SIGNIFICANCE OF HOSEA 6:2

AS FURTHER VERIFICATION of this teaching, Rabbi Bechai stated, "When Messiah comes, the six thousand years will be completed. Then the seventh day shall go on, a genuine Sabbath and eternal life."

Rabbi Katina said, "The seventh millennium shall be the thousand years of remission that God alone may be exalted in that day."

The Jewish teachers have never believed that the world would end with the advent of the year 2000 and years immediately following. That would be a period when the affairs of earth would at long last be governed with tranquillity, blessedness, peace, and rest—the promised social environment when Messiah would appear and rule.

Hosea 6:2 is a pivotal verse at this juncture. The prophet states, "After two days will he revive us: in the third day he will raise us up, and we shall live in his sight." Here is the significance of this Scripture. In the year 70

> . . . almost two thousand years passed before the Jews of the diaspora became a nation.

A.D. Titus, the Roman general, marched to Jerusalem, murdered a million of God's people, drove the rest to the far-flung corners of the earth, thus disallowing the Jews from possessing their homeland for centuries. In fact, almost two thousand years passed before the Jews of the diaspora became a nation.

## FOUR GROUPS OF BELIEVERS

WITH THAT BRIEF background we return to the text, "After two days will He revive us." That day of "reviving" was May 14, 1948, when Israel became a nation—almost at the end of the "two days." The rest of the passage reads, "in the third day (soon after the coming of 2000 A.D.) He will raise us up, and we shall live in His sight." That is the resurrection that takes place in Daniel 12:2: "And many of them that sleep in the dust of the earth shall awake, some to everlasting life, and some to shame and everlasting contempt."

But there's more. When the King returns to set up His kingdom, He will bring multitudes with Him, those who were previously raptured. That is the profound significance of Jude verse 14, "And Enoch also, the seventh from Adam, prophesied of these, saying, Behold, the Lord cometh with ten thousands of his saints." This is group number one.

Those in group two are the Jewish saints of Old Testament times whom God raises up. These are the people referred to in Daniel 12:2.

Group three includes the multitude who have died during the tribulation period for their faith in Christ. They became children of God through the redemption of Christ's sacrifice for them, and during that time, refused the mark of the beast (Revelation 13:15). Because of their love for Christ and their stubborn faithfulness to God, Revelation 20:4 says, "And I saw thrones, and they sat upon them, and judgment was given unto them: and I saw the souls of them that were beheaded for the witness of Jesus, and for the word of God, and which had not worshipped the beast, neither his image, neither had received his mark upon their foreheads, or in their hands; and they lived and reigned with Christ a thousand years."

Note especially the last part of that verse—"and they lived and reigned with Christ a thousand years." That is their spiritual coup de grace. They are now rewarded for their faith and faithfulness with a gift of a thousand-year reign with their Savior and Lord.

Group four are those described in Matthew 25, verses 31 to 46, where God judges the nations. Those who've received Messiah as their own, and have shown respect to the Jews because of their love for Messiah, are allowed to enter the kingdom. Verse 46 reads, "Then shall the King say unto them on his right hand, Come, ye blessed of my Father, inherit the kingdom prepared for you from the foundation of the world."

> "Come, ye blessed of my Father, inherit the kingdom prepared for you from the foundation of the world."
> —Matthew 25:46

They are coming from heaven. They're being brought up from the ground, from the Jewish faith, from Old Testament times. They're being raised from the earth because they died during the tribulation hour, and they're now being divided in Matthew 25 into all of these four groups for one special purpose. . . . to go into the kingdom of earth.

## RESURRECTION: A JEWISH THEME

HISTORICALLY, the theme of resurrection has been a familiar topic for rabbis, and it continues to be a recurrent thesis in their teaching and in their schools. It is this resurrection of God's people that will be among the most significant of all events during the millennium period. It will be as Rabbi Eliazar said, "Messiah's days shall be one thousand years, for it is written 'a day in God's sight is a thousand years.'"

Rabbi Jose agrees when he underlines the message of Rabbi Eliazar by adding that "Messiah's days are the days of restitution for Israel, and are one thousand years." Many do not realize how closely Christians are actually aligned in their theology with orthodox Jews and rabbis. For centuries, those of the Jewish faith have believed in a literal, not-to-be-argued-against, thousand years of Messiah's reign.

For many Christians this theme is captivating, yet largely unstudied. That's why I encourage those with a desire to know more about the Jewish historical position to get a copy of the *Jewish Encyclopedia,* or *Encyclopedia Judaica,* and look up the subjects, *Millennium* and *Chiliasm.* It's all there—the teaching of a seven-day period. Six thousand years of history—four thousand years from Adam to Christ—and two thousand years from the historical Christ until the year 2000 or shortly thereafter, after which the Messiah will appear during those final thousand years. It is a seminal part of Jewish history. And the Jews are not alone in their belief of this millennial event.

## THE CHRISTIAN FATHERS AGREE

THAT THE "Christian fathers" and historians of Christianity are in basic agreement with Jewish scholars on the nature of the millennium and the Messiah's reign for one thousand years on earth is confirmed in numerous ways. Barnabas, in the Epistle of Barnabas—an apocraphal New Testament letter cited by Clemens, Alexandrinus, Origen, Eusebius, Jerome, and many ancient fathers—said that in six thousand years the Lord will bring all things to an end, for with Him, one day is as a thousand years.

Barnabas did not say this would then be the end of the earth as we know it. Rather, that it would be only the beginning of a thousand-year reign, and that the seventh day would be millennial rest. Saint Bartholomew taught the same truth. Both were great men of God and true stalwarts of the Christian faith, and they shared this teaching directly from the New Testament, from passages such as 2 Peter 3:8, which reads,

> "But, beloved, be not ignorant of this one thing, that one day *is* with the Lord as a thousand years, and a thousand years as one day."

Bishop Hippolytus also was in agreement. As was Victorinus, Bishop of Peteau, who penned a commentary on the Apocalypse around 27 A.D. He wrote: "The true and just Sabbath shall be observed in the seventh millennium of years when Christ with His elect shall reign." John E. Walvoord has written, "Practically all students of the early church agree that premillennialism . . . was the view held by many in the apostolic age."

As we said in chapter 1, God's Word is literally true, and we do ourselves a great spiritual disservice not to immerse ourselves in the clear, irrefutable counsel of the Word of Truth. Yet, nothing seems to be more unclear to Christians than the how, when, and who of the end times and the approaching millennium. Saint Irenaeus said in 140 A.D. "For in as many days as their world was made, in so many thousand years shall it be concluded, for the day of the Lord is a thousand years, and in six days created things were completed."

If this is truth, then why do so many choose to explain away God's clear message to His people? This is a question we will answer in several ways throughout the remainder of this book. Meanwhile, with this brief historic background in place, let's revisit some timely events which remind us that the millennial clock is ticking, giving us even more bedrock reasons to be vigilant, and to know and understand the times as we count down to eternity.

## WARS AND RUMORS OF WARS

BY THE YEAR 2000, according to U.S. intelligence sources, as many as twenty-four Third World nations—countries such as Libya, Iraq, Syria, and Iran—will have acquired long-range ballistic missiles. Half of them may have a nuclear capability.

That means it won't be just Russia and China who threaten the United States and the free world. Moammar Gadhafy or Saddam Hussein may be able to launch a nuclear assault on the United States, and America will be defenseless to save itself and millions of lives.

Furthermore, there are now forty countries that have in their arsenals cruise-type missiles capable of hitting U.S. cities if fired from a ship or submarine. Some can be fitted with chemical warheads, and the threat will be considerably worse within a decade. Even the African nation of Ghana has begun a nuclear research program that could lead to the development of a warhead.

International intelligence expert Don McAlvany points out that all the citizens of

> . . . There are now forty countries that have . . . cruise-type missiles capable of hitting U.S. cities if fired from a ship or submarine.

Russia, China, and Switzerland have nuclear sheltering. "What do they know that *we* don't know?" he asks. Good question.

Most Americans, polls show, are still unaware that no missile defense system has been currently deployed to protect major U.S. cities or even military bases from missile attack. At present, there is no way we can stop even one ballistic missile fired at the United States.

## U.S. READINESS JEOPARDIZED

AT PRESENT, the U.S. government is pursuing a policy of deploying ground-based interceptors that could protect a handful of territories overseas, but offer little or no protection to Americans. The cost for this program is $14.9 billion dollars. Meanwhile, General Daniel Graham says a space-based missile defense system could protect all Americans and our allies at a cost of only $12 billion. The question is this: Will American leadership wake up to the realities of what could be impending disaster? Unfortunately, there is ample evidence that it will not—and that the United States may one day fall victim to a nuclear first strike.

While the United States "plays games," Russian President Boris Yeltsin has broadened the powers of the successor agency of the KGB to allow searches without warrants, to legalize electronic surveillance, and to revive gathering of foreign intelligence.

## THE U.S. ARMY ENGAGES IN KIDS' PLAY

THOUGH THE U.S. is spending the same amount on defense as it was in the 1980s, military strength has been severely reduced. Army divisions have dropped from twenty-eight to twenty; air force wings fell from thirty-six to twenty-two; the navy budgeted for 387 ships, down from 568, and troop strength went from 2.2 million to 1.6 million.

In addition, a Defense Department initiative to involve troops in community work could be a further setback to military readiness. The army is dropping surplus battle tanks in favor of a program to bolster natural reefs; the marine corps reserves are building a bridge in Georgia; army reservists are conducting a summer camp for kids in Pennsylvania. Is this what an army is supposed to do? We need to do more than stand watch in defense of a sandbox!

### ISRAEL'S ECONOMY IN SHAMBLES

THE ISRAELI economy continues to find itself in desperate straits. Business leaders fear unemployment and even higher interest rates in the days ahead. "We are one minute before an economic catastrophe, and the feeling is that the government, the Bank of Israel, and the public live in a paradise of fools," said Dan Propper, president of Israel's Manufacturers Association.

### HARVESTING ORGANS FROM BABIES

THE AMERICAN Medical Association (AMA) is promoting the idea of harvesting organs from live anencephalic babies. Rabbi Lester Frazin of Congregation B'nai Israel in Sacramento, California, likened "experimenting or harvesting organs from living human beings as reminiscent of Nazi Germany's experimentation."

When one has completed toying with human life, what else can possibly remain for scientific investigation?

### U.S. NOW SEES CHINA PERIL

CHINA IS A HUGE country, with a population of some 1.2 billion. However, the magnitude of this nation is also a two-edged sword for its leaders: the masses must be fed, clothed, and put to work. On the other hand, the sheer numbers of men, women, and children also make the country a loose cannon that could aim virtually any of its desires at anyone, anywhere, at any time. Chairman Mao once said that China could easily lose half its population, and still win its battles with the enemy. Whether or not at the time he was blowing Marxist smoke, there's little denial of that truth today.

At present, U.S. intelligence agency strategic planners are beginning to get nervous about the growing economic power of this once-dormant Asian giant that is no longer sleeping. When intelligence sources search for historical precedents for such rapid growth in totalitarian nations, there are some ominous parallels—Germany in the 1880s and Japan in the 1920s. China is currently testing its missiles in what are international waters. But the tests are so close to Taiwan that they are terrifying the small island nation, which is regarded as a "renegade province" by Beijing, and therefore Chinese territory.

## SWEATY PALMS IN THE DOD

"I'M WORRIED, I really am," said a China specialist at the Defense Department's national War College. "I had assumed that when China's revolutionary elite passed away, the venom of Marxism-Leninism would be removed from China's defense policies. But that venom has been replaced by extreme nationalism." China's defense budget, adjusted for inflation, has increased by about 40 percent over the past five years, while Russian and American military budgets have either been cut, or remained flat.

> China's defense budget . . . has increased about 40 percent over the past five years. . . .

In addition, China is buying massive amounts of sophisticated weaponry from Russia and other countries. Annual economic growth is approaching a staggering 12 percent. Beijing is also making new territorial claims over huge tracts of ocean and over disputed islands.

What does God's Word say about the boiling cauldron of

geopolitical events in China? Revelation 9:16–18 speaks as closely to this issue as any portion of Scripture:

> "And the number of the army of the horsemen *were* two hundred thousand thousand: and I heard the number of them. And thus I saw the horses in the vision, and them that sat on them, having breastplates of fire, and of jacinth, and brimstone: and the heads of the horses *were* as the heads of lions; and out of their mouths issued fire and smoke and brimstone. By these three was the third part of men killed, by the fire, and by the smoke, and by the brimstone, which issued out of their mouths."

## THE KINGS OF THE EAST?

ACCORDING TO A recent public opinion poll in Japan, 66 percent of the Japanese people believe that China will be the country's most important partner in the future. Revelation 16:12 says, "And the sixth angel poured out his vial upon the great river Euphrates; and the water thereof was dried up, that the way of the kings of the east might be prepared."

Meanwhile, the Department for the Study of National Conditions of the Chinese Academy of Sciences has set the decade beginning 2020 as the target date for China becoming the world's number one economy. Other forecasters say China's economy will equal that of the U.S. within ten years.

Do you have difficulty believing that the world as we know it is rapidly drawing to a close? If you do, then the remaining chapters of this book are especially written for you. Because the compelling evidence for the approach of the end times is mounting by the second—something we will discover in chapter 3. We will be further awakened from our complacency and slumber, realizing that geopolitically there is more international instability than ever, an insecurity and anxiety best demonstrated by the growling and pawing of the great Russian bear that is no longer in hibernation.

"I think we are seeing the actual manifestation and materialization of forces of good and evil in direct combat. We're on that battle ground, we're in the middle of that crossfire right now."

—MICHAEL BROWN

# THE BEAR NO LONGER SLEEPS

**T**HE COLD WAR IS OVER, right? The former Soviet Union no longer poses a danger to the community of nations, we're told. Therefore, why bother defending ourselves from intercontinental ballistic missiles? We simply don't need to. And an army? A waste of time. There are less stressful things for our men and women in uniform to do than remain in a perpetual state of war readiness.

For what it's worth, that is the conventional wisdom of the day—that Mother Russia is an innocent, cuddly, sleepy bear, uninterested in global expansion—too soft and comfortable in hibernation to entertain thoughts of organizing an international threat. Further, we're told that any report of a "new red tide sweeping across nations" is wild-eyed doomsday rhetoric, propagated by the fearful and uninformed. The threat from Russia is gone, we're assured. Well, is it? I don't think so.

### HARD-LINERS POSED FOR RETURN TO POWER

*WORLD PRESS REVIEW* reports:
"The New Red Tide: The Commissars Are Back." The *Globe and*

*Mail* writes that "after a lifetime of dogged persistence and shrewd maneuvering, Gennady Zyuganov has found himself (before Yeltsin's victory on July 3, 1996) on the threshold of power. In Russia's parliamentary elections ... Zyuaganov's revitalized Communists scored the biggest victory of any party in the country."

While continuing to devastate the majority of its people with poverty, while proclaiming peaceful "partnerships," Russia continues to lull the West into a complacent defense strategy. Yet, the Russian military machine grinds on.

The British journal *Aerospace* revealed that "the technology to detect multi-billion-dollar American Stealth bombers was recently displayed in London. The cold war might be over, but it is the Russians who have developed the capability to detect Stealth bombers, [which were the pride of U.S. air defenses, so crucial in winning the Gulf War]." Incidentally, this new de-stealthing technology is now on the market for sale in fifty-one countries.

> **. . . Russia has Israel in her gun sights.**

Although the media continues to play up peace negotiations between Israel and the Arab nations, Russia has Israel in her gun sights. This will lead to an invasion when war is anything but expected. Serious students of Bible prophecy have long expected this military move where nearly all the Arab nations will be allies of Russia—with their primary purpose being to take Israel.

This "land to the north" will be marching to the Middle East to help herself to the spoils of battle. Russia will be pleased to cooperate in the conquest of Israel, knowing that when its military forces overrun the Middle East, it will control all the wealth in the region—including Arab oil and Israeli national resources. Add to these riches the mineral wealth of the Dead Sea (two trillion dollars worth), as well as the wealth being generated in Israel through industry and agriculture, and there will be great spoils of war indeed.

Even as you read this chapter, 1,400 factories throughout Russia are manufacturing weaponry for a future war. If Russia pursues its military objectives, these arms will be used. Despite official claims that the Red Army has been downsized to 2.3 million, intelligence sources tell us the real number is closer to five million men and women in Russian uniform. As if that were not enough soldiery, the Russians also have conscripted one million KGB agents to serve as interior guards. And there's more.

Moscow has reinstated the military draft, and the resurgent Russian bear is spending some 43 percent of its gross national product on the military, all the while feigning peace and love. Let's take a look at the real Russia—the one the internationalists and many of a politically liberal persuasion would prefer you never see.

Russia has failed to implement any of the nuclear security and arms inspection agreements announced by President Bill Clinton and President Boris Yeltsin at their well-publicized summit. This has resulted in the suspension of mutual inspections and data exchanges. In fact, Russia has developed and deployed a doomsday machine called the "dead hand," a computerized system that can automatically fire its nuclear arsenal if military commanders are dead or unable to direct the battle. Is the Russian bear *really* sleeping?

## PLAGUE SPRAY AND NUCLEAR STOCKPILES

LARGELY UNKNOWN to the outside world, we now have information that the Russian military, in defiance of its own president, has been secretly developing biological weapons of mass destruction, including a "super-plague" for which the West has no antidote. The plague is so powerful that just 440 pounds sprayed from planes or using airburst bombs could kill up to 500,000 people.

Despite signing agreements that banned such activity, Russia is still developing and manufacturing the most deadly chemical agents known to man, including "Novichok," which is reportedly ten times more toxic to humans than the present deadliest nerve gas, VX. The bear is more than stirring in its cave. It's wide awake, and it knows what it is doing.

Not only is Russia manufacturing record amounts of conventional weaponry for its own use, it is also exporting more than ever, in part to finance an even greater arms buildup. Russia still has some 30,000 nuclear weapons. And a reliable intelligence source reports that at least forty-six nuclear warheads—some in the megaton range—are missing from former Soviet stockpiles. Could this be the result of gross bureaucratic incompetence? Or is someone profiting by selling rogue nations nuclear arms? I think the answer is obvious.

Due to the leakage of warheads and weapons-grade nuclear material from Russia and other former Soviet countries, top intelligence experts now say the threat of a nuclear terrorist attack is greater than at any time since the height of the cold war. When one adds the unprecedented political instability Russia is facing to this already highly explosive militaristic equation, a darkened socio-political sky becomes darker still. Yet, the West remains unprepared for what could be the greatest sneak attack in history.

Since 1993, Russia has been moving aggressively toward a full modernization of its strategic nuclear arsenal. Its new military doctrine emphasizes reliance on nuclear weapons more heavily than ever. This modernization campaign includes building a new bomber, the Sukhoi T-60; upgrading its Typhoon strategic ballistic missile submarines; laying the keels of a new missile-sub class; and launching a new mobile intercontinental ballistic missile, the TOPOL-M.

> ... The West remains unprepared for what could be the greatest sneak attack in history.

The executive branch of the United States government has recently made a secret concession in the interpretation of the Strategic Arms Reduction Treaty that will allow Moscow to move its mobile SS-

ICBMs anywhere in the world—or sell them to countries such as China, Cuba, Libya, North Korea, and Syria. This can be done as long as they are reclassified as "space launchers," and accompanied by Russian personnel.

Despite protests from the United States, Russia is planning to sell substantial amounts of weapons-grade enriched uranium to operators of nuclear research reactors in Europe, a move certain to result in a further proliferation of nuclear arms. Yeltsin may not be the "peaceful" man he portrays himself to be: After all, he appointed intelligence chief Yevgeny Primakov as foreign minister.

## NEW LEADERS . . . OLD IDEAS

PRIMAKOV HAPPENS to be a thirty-year member of the Communist Party with strong ties to the Arab world, including Iraq's Saddam Hussein. Primakov opposed the allied military effort to drive Iraq out of Kuwait, and continues to be pro-Arab as he further muscles his way into the Arab camp. Most recently the head of the spy agency formerly known as the KBG, Primakov is decidedly anti-West and anti-conservative.

Does it sound as if the Russian bear is really dancing to a new tune? Or do you read the reports as I do, with suspicion that there is more going on than the casual eye can see? Even more disquieting is that while Moscow is lurching back toward totalitarianism and militarism, individuals with great political clout in the United States have been cutting secret deals that could well cripple America's ability to protect its own territory and people from incoming missiles.

## THE CARTELS ARE BOSS

AND WHAT ABOUT the much-debated political reforms set in motion by Yeltsin? It's obvious now that Russia will not vote its way into a free and democratic future.

All the leading contenders to the Russian "throne" have stated publicly that they want to rebuild the Russian military machine even more rapidly than it is currently being resurrected. They have also voiced their intentions to end the experimentation with privatization of the economy. In a nod toward being "reformist," they give only lip service to their pledge to fight organized crime and government corruption.

It's like what a wise person once told me: "When it's all said and done, there is usually more *said* than *done!*"

What appears to be emerging in the new Russia is not so much a rebirth of Soviet-style Communism as a 1990s brand of national socialism—even fascism. International intelligence experts and foreign policy analysts see Russia being dominated increasingly by powerful elite cartels in major sectors of the economy in the months and years ahead.

Under a fascist system of rule, authoritarian leaders would work hand-in-hand with these interest groups, rather than attempt to deprive them of power as a traditional all-powerful Communist government might. This strange alliance may have the outward manifestation of cooperation, while it actually is a carefully orchestrated plan to usurp, and maintain power.

For example, organized crime now controls 50 to 80 percent of Russia's banks, and has turned the country into one of the world's major money-laundering centers. More than half of all Russian capital, and 80 percent of voting shares in privatized businesses pass into the possession of criminal structures. The Russian Mafia rules more than 40,000 businesses in the country. It is all beginning to make the criminal activity of Al Capone and his Chicago hoods look like an innocent fist-fight in the park. And speaking of thugs . . .

### RUSSIA WILL RISE, SAYS GENERAL LEBED

POWERFUL RUSSIAN General Alexander Lebed, Russian security chief, said, "Russia is not to be taken lightly. Russia will be respected." In a policy statement titled "A New Approach to Problems of National Security," Lebed wrote that in Yeltsin's second term as president "countries will be classified in order of their friendship to Russia."

Regarding NATO, he has said, "No one will push Russia into a corner." He also has said such expansion could trigger World War III.

Brookings Institute's Russian analyst, Jerry Hough, wrote in the *Moscow Times:* "Events in Russia now are probably out of American control. . . . In the future, the United States is likely to look at the Yeltsin-Lebed alliance with far less enthusiasm than it does at present" (just after the election).

In his autobiography *The Last Play for the South,* Russian hard-liner Vladimir Zhirinovsky muses about Russian soldiers massing for a last great crusade to the Indian Ocean and the Mediterranean. For Zhirinovsky, this is not fiction. It is a prediction of real events that could conceivably occur were he, or those like him, ever to assume power.

> "Russia is not to be taken lightly."
> —Russian General Alexander Lebed

In an interview after his first big showing in Russia's parliamentary elections, Zhirinovsky painted an apocalyptic picture of conflicts between Iran and Iraq, Azerbaijan and Armenia, Pakistan and India, and Turkish intervention in Transcaucasus. Here are his words:

> "These conflicts will make a hell of these regions, with war raging for ten to fifteen years. Cities and roads will be destroyed, epidemics will explode, millions will die, and neither America nor the United Nations will be able to do anything about it. The world community will beg us to save what remains of those peoples in Central Asia, the Middle East, and the Indian Ocean coast. We will be obliged to send our boys there, and our army will then appear on the coast of the Indian Ocean "

A sleeping bear? Harmless? Benign? Hardly.

## "NOT ONE HAPPY DAY"

MAKE NO MISTAKE about it, Zhirinovsky is an embittered, miserable, unhappy, angry, insecure, power-hungry man with totalitarian ambitions. He's been compared to Adolph Hitler, with those parallels easy to see, even though he says his dream of national socialism was discredited by the Nazis.

He's a product of seventy years of Communist oppression, and has capitalized on the misery of working people in Russia to propel himself into political prominence. His autobiography provides frightening glimpses of this man's evil potential. As have so many other demagogues before him, he revels in his own humiliations and depravation—both real and imagined.

You may have read the following interview. It is honest. Forthcoming. Frank. And frightening. Again, in Zhirinovsky's own words:

> "I was denied the most elementary family coziness, human warmth. Life itself forced me to suffer from the very day, the moment, the instant of my birth. Society could give me nothing. Two months before her death, my mother would tell me, 'Volodya, there's nothing to remember, not one happy day.'"

Not only is the bear stirring, but it is an unhappy bear, with hatred and revenge on its mind.

> **Not only is the bear stirring, but it is an unhappy bear. . . .**

And what has been the West's reaction to the rise of Zhirinovsky? While the rhetoric has been forceful, there has been little change in the defensive posture of the United States, which continues unilaterally to disarm and dismantle the early stages of its Strategic Defense Initiative. "No American, no thinking citizen of the world who reads such comments [by Zhirinovsky] could fail to be concerned," President Clinton once said about this would-be leader's harsh campaign claims.

I'm pleased that United States political leadership is concerned, but concern alone will not deter Zhirinovsky or the hegemonic ambitions of the Russian nationalists he represents. Meanwhile, official U.S. policy toward Russia remains ostrich-like, to say the least.

## WE KNOW WHERE THIS IS TAKING US

ALL THIS IS LEADING up to precisely what the Hebrew prophets predicted hundreds of years before the birth of Christ. Ezekiel 38 and 39 refer to a time in the near future when a powerful, reborn Russia betrays the leader of a world government based in Europe and, with alliances created with countries such as Germany, Iran, Iraq, Libya, Turkey, Egypt, Syria, and some of the former Soviet republics, launches an all-out military invasion of Israel. (See Daniel 11:40–45; Ezekiel 38:5–6; Psalm 53:4–8.) Ezekiel 38:4 says, "And I will turn thee back, and put hooks into thy jaws, and I will bring thee forth, and all thine army, horses and horsemen, all of them clothed with all sorts of armour, even a great company with bucklers and shields, all of them handling swords."

This attack comes after a European world leader—the first true global dictator—makes a covenant of peace with Israel, pledging to protect the Jewish state against all aggressors. Russia then takes the leadership in fomenting a rebellion against this world ruler in the form of a blitzkrieg-style surprise attack on the Middle East. But it is Russia that is surprised—caught off guard that its overwhelming power, might, and influence are repelled. What follows is the bloodiest war in the history of mankind—all condensed in a relatively short three-and-one-half-year period, climaxed by the physical return of our Lord Jesus Christ to rule over the earth.

## THE BIBLE SAYS . . .

BUT BEFORE CHRIST returns and brings peace and order to the world, many of those fearsome weapons of mass destruction I mentioned earlier will be used. How do we know this? Because

God's Word makes it clear for those with eyes open to see, and ears ready to hear. There are specific references to an unquenchable fire associated with this war in Psalm 97:3, "A fire goeth before him, and burneth up his enemies round about."

Isaiah 66:15 says, "For, behold, the LORD will come with fire, and with his chariots like a whirlwind, to render his anger with fury, and his rebuke with flames of fire."

Ezekiel 20:47 states, "And say to the forest of the south, Hear the word of the LORD; Thus saith the Lord GOD; Behold, I will kindle a fire in thee, and it shall devour every green tree in thee, and every dry tree: the flaming flame shall not be quenched, and all faces from the south to the north shall be burned therein."

Zephaniah 1:18 reads, "Neither their silver nor their gold shall be able to deliver them in the day of the LORD's wrath; but the whole land shall be devoured by the fire of his jealousy: for he shall make even a speedy riddance of all them that dwell in the land."

Malachi 4:1 reminds us, "For, behold, the day cometh, that shall burn as an oven; and all the proud, yea, and all that do wickedly, shall be stubble: and the day that cometh shall burn them up, saith the LORD of hosts, that it shall leave them neither root nor branch."

Revelation 8:7 says, "The first angel sounded, and there followed hail and fire mingled with blood, and they were cast upon the earth: and the third part of trees was burnt up, and all green grass was burnt up."

But as instructive and informative as these portions of Scripture are, none are as relevant as the verses found in Joel 2:1–31. In verses 1 and 2, the prophet says, "Let all the inhabitants of the land tremble, for the day of the Lord cometh, for *it is* nigh at hand, A day of darkness and of gloominess, a day of clouds and thick darkness."

Why? Because an enemy, Russia, is coming from the north to attack Israel. Verse 3 then describes a fire that devours everything before the invading hordes. "A fire devoureth before them; and behind them a flame burneth: the land is as the garden of Eden before them, and behind them a desolate wilderness; yea, and nothing shall escape them."

Verse 10 says "The earth shall quake before them; the heavens shall tremble: the sun and the moon shall be dark, and the stars shall withdraw their shining."

In verse 20 we read, "But I will remove far off from you the northern *army,* and will drive him into a land barren and desolate, with his face toward the east sea, and his hinder part

> "For, behold, the day cometh, that shall burn as an oven."
> —Malachi 4:1

toward the utmost sea, and his stink shall come up, and his ill savour shall come up, because he hath done great things."

Verses 30–31 continue, "And I will shew wonders in the heavens and in the earth, blood, and fire, and pillars of smoke. The sun shall be turned into darkness, and the moon into blood."

Finally, Ezekiel 39:6 says, "I will rain fire upon Magog."

## THE BEAR SLUMBERS NO MORE

GIVEN WHAT WE have just read, it should come as no surprise to learn that some Russians have been boasting of another new weapon in their arsenal. It's called the Elipton bomb. This state-of-the-art instrument of torture destroys people—literally dissolves them—but leaves their human structures intact. The Bible predicts, in Zechariah 14:12, "Their flesh shall consume away while they stand upon their feet, and their eyes shall consume away in their holes, and their tongue shall consume away in their mouth."

Is this not precisely what the Elipton bomb is designed to do?

When it comes to Russia's intentions and capabilities, I'm afraid the West has been fooling itself. The bear is not in hibernation. It is awake, hungry, and ready to pounce on the world, just as God's Word has prophesied. But even while the bear stirs from its alleged slumber, the United States and Western Europe continue to make policy based more on wishful thinking than on strategic realities.

"It has been the steadfast conviction of Americans after each great conflict in this century—two world wars, Korea, Vietnam, and the cold war—that we could finally get back to normal times, could at least turn to domestic pursuits," recalls Robert Gates, former director of the Central Intelligence Agency. Gates is right.

As a nation we fight, make up, and hope for the best. It's naiveté of the highest order. Americans have always considered war and conflict as aberrations of normalcy, so four times in this century—1918, 1945, 1953, and 1975—we have precipitously disarmed ourselves, declared a peace dividend, and attempted to turn inward. But, each time, our hopes have been dashed against the rocks of political reality. Is history ready to repeat itself?

Would that the world's leaders spent more time in God's Word than in intelligence briefings; and more hours asking God's counsel in the prayer room, rather than playing battle games in the war room.

But what is happening around us is simply setting us up for the cataclysmic events that will take place during the next millennium. If we were to speak of our world's condition in nautical terms, we would have to say that the captain is uncertain of his direction, the crew is untrained and naive, the boat is leaking, the once-faithful compass has failed, and the ship of state is headed for the worst shipwreck humankind has ever known. And Russia will play a key role in the final chapter of the demise of what we know as planet earth.

> . . . Russia will play a key role in the final chapter of the demise of what we know as planet earth.

## IT SHOULD BE NO SURPRISE

RUSSIA IS DESTINED to light the fuse in the final world war. And the signs of the times indicate that these events are not far off in the distant future. The world is on the brink. The only Good News is that Christ's return to earth follows this war. The Jewish writing *Avoda Zara* 3b states: "The war of Gog and Magog occurs just before Messiah appears."

When, exactly, will this day come? No one can say with certainty. The Bible reminds us that He will come "as a thief in the night." His ultimate appearing will be a surprise, but the fact that He will one day appear should come as no surprise to the one who knows Jesus Christ as Savior and Lord.

But before that grand event, other worldwide physical and social phenomena will take place on earth that will continue to set the stage for that great day. These will be events that will affect all of mankind—from the farmer in America's midwest, to the oil tycoon in Kuwait, to the school teacher in London, to everyone—everywhere—in between.

One of the most important and intriguing events of all will be the growing, aggressive international threat of a militant Islam. This, complete with old enemies coming together to form the foundation of the coalition of nations, will join Russia in the invasion of Israel as described in Ezekiel 38.

**4**

## THE ISLAMIC THREAT: GOOD-BYE, ALI BABA

THE *ARABIAN NIGHTS,* also known as *The Thousand and One Nights,* is a vast collection of stories, mostly of Arabian, Indian, or Persian origins. They were written in the Arabic language sometime between the fourteenth and sixteenth centuries.

The basic tale turns on the woman-hating King Schahriah who, after his queen's open infidelity, marries a different woman each night, and then slays her the next morning, thus ensuring her faithfulness. One bride, Shaharazad, however, enchants the king with a series of tales that last a thousand and one nights, withholding the ending of each story until the next night. With this clever ploy, she saves her life. Most people in the West have enjoyed these ornately plotted stories for years, the main ones being "The History of Aladdin, or the Wonderful Lamp," "The History of Sinbad the Sailor," and "The History of Ali Baba and the Forty Thieves."

### "OPEN SESAME"

WITH THE STAGE SET in the warm sands of the exotic Middle

East, these narratives of intrigue provide readers worldwide with a romanticized view of well-fed, well-heeled sheiks. Theirs was a society of wealth beyond measure, ever-available harems adorning ornate palaces and not-so-humble tents of the desert lords. All the harmless tales recounted a glorious past. Nothing threatening. Just for fun. At some time most of us even learned—and played with—the magic password, "Open Sesame," that was uttered by Ali Baba after he accidentally witnessed thieves stashing stolen treasure in a secret cave.

But that was then. Today, the romance is over. And you can forget "Open Sesame," because it will take more than two magic words to open the hearts and minds of those who espouse the name of Allah, and believe that Muhammad is his prophet. Because while the fundamental teachings of Muhammad remain unchanged, Islam's religious, political, and economic powers have grown so enormous that the foundations of the region, and now the world, are being shaken.

Historically, the area in question has been called the Fertile Crescent, a name given to that part of the Middle East where the earliest known civilizations on earth began. The region bends like an arc from the Nile Valley of Egypt north along the coast of the Mediterranean Sea. It then winds its way east and south through the Tigris and Euphrates valleys, on to the head of the Persian Gulf where it passes through present-day Israel, Lebanon, Syria, Iraq, and western Iran.

Once known largely for its deserts, camels, over-nourished potentates, and tales of *The Thousand and One Nights,* the Fertile Crescent is now recognized for its money, Mercedes, mansions, oil, political power, and, by some, the key role it will play in world history as we approach 2001 and the edge of eternity. To ignore the world of Islam is to court disaster. To pretend that a militant Islamic fundamentalism is not a major piece of the eschatological puzzle is a stubborn refusal to understand the times.

## ISLAM IS LIFE . . . LIFE IS ISLAM

IT IS NOW estimated there are between 750 million and 1.2 billion Muslims in the world today. Observers generally agree that the number of Muslims worldwide is increasing by some twenty-five million per year. If this is an accurate number, there will be a 250-million increase during the final decade of this century. This significant expansion, due largely to the general population growth in Asia and Africa, is gradually lowering the numerical difference between Christians and Muslims, whose combined totals make up almost 50 percent of the world's population.

> For the Muslim, Islam is life, and life is Islam.

As a religion, Islam brings together personal faith and piety, and promotes a sacred doctrine followed by fervent believers. It teaches a way of life, and an unalterable code of ethics. It leans heavily on its ancient culture, has codified a defiant set of laws, and promotes its own understanding of the purpose of government. For the Muslim, Islam is life, and life is Islam.

Today, the threat of Islamic fundamentalism is so enormous that it increasingly calls the shots in the region, has the clout to sponsor international terrorism, and plays its "oil card" again and again while the world panics. Devoted Islamics continue to invade every corner of the world with the message of Mohammad. If you don't believe Islam is making an international impact, just count the number of mosques being built in major European and American cities. Consider London, for example, where you'll have no trouble finding an Islamic place of worship.

Most observers, Christian or not, recognize that a radical Islam will be the most disquieting, threatening player in the continual destabilization of world affairs from now into the next millennium. Let's take a series of snapshots of what is happening in the world of Islam today, and see how these events compare—or at least line up—with what has been predicted in Scripture.

## Iran's Arrangement with Russia

IRAN HAS MADE a deal with Russia not to make trouble in the former Soviet republics of Central Asia in exchange for Moscow's support of Tehran's designs on dominating the Persian Gulf. The latest evidence of this pact has been the civil war in Tajikistan. Islam rebels are trying to topple the government of former Communists in a bloody conflict that has now claimed more than 50,000 lives.

Iran is a natural ally for the Islamic rebels. Yet, Tehran is making peace with the regime in power. Tajik President Imomali Rakhmonov recently announced he had secured a ten-million-dollar loan from Iran and signed twelve cooperation agreements. Iran and Russia form the lynch pin of the Armageddon coalition that, according to the Bible, will invade the Middle East just prior to the return of Jesus Christ. (See Ezekiel 38.)

## Palestine Police Force

IN GRANTING LIMITED autonomy to the Palestinians in the Gaza Strip, Israel may be getting much more than it bargained for. Originally, Yasser Arafat's Palestinian Authority employed 9,000 policemen to patrol the streets of the Jewish-occupied Arab territory. In only a few months, that number skyrocketed to 25,000—a veritable standing army far exceeding what was allotted in the agreement with Israel.

Read Psalm 83 with this current event in mind:

> "Keep not thou silence, O God: hold not thy peace, and be not still, O God. For, lo, thine enemies make a tumult: and they that hate thee have lifted up the head. They have taken crafty counsel against thy people, and consulted against thy hidden ones. They have said, Come, and let us cut them off from *being* a nation; that the name of Israel may be no more in remembrance. For they have consulted together with one consent:

they are confederate against thee: The tabernacles of Edom, and the Ishmaelites; of Moab, and the Hagarenes; Gebal, and Ammon, and Amalek; the Philistines with the inhabitants of Tyre; Assur also is joined with them: they have helped the children of Lot. Selah. Do *unto* them as unto the Midianites; as to Sisera, as *to* Jabin, at the brook of Kison: *Which* perished at Endor: they became *as* dung for the earth. Make their nobles like Oreb, and like Zeeb: yea, all their princes as Zebah, and as Zalmunna: Who said, Let us take to ourselves the houses of God in possession. O my God, make them like a wheel; as the stubble before the wind. As the fire burneth a wood, and as the flame setteth the mountains on fire; So persecute them with thy tempest, and make them afraid with thy storm. Fill their faces with shame; that they may seek thy name, O Lord. Let them be confounded and troubled for ever; yea, let them be put to shame, and perish: That *men* may know that thou, whose name alone is JEHOVAH, *art* the most high over all the earth."

## CRISIS IN SYRIA TALKS

MEANWHILE, PEACE TALKS continue to bog down between Israel and Syria over the issue of security on the Golan Heights. The Peres government was prepared to hand over the strategic mountain area to Damascus in exchange for an agreement to allow Jerusalem to maintain early-warning stations to monitor troop and artillery movements. Syria refuses not only to allow Israel to hold on to such listening posts, but also to allow third parties—such as the United Nations—to man them.

Here's the problem. Israel knows that Syria still dreams of invading Israel one day, and wants the element of surprise added to its already formidable military arsenal. Although this may seem to be a small item on a larger political agenda, the Bible has spoken through the prophet Isaiah about what is starting to happen before our eyes. In Isaiah 17:1 we read, "The burden of Damascus. Behold, Damascus is taken away from *being* a city, and it shall be a ruinous heap."

## TURKEY: HOW LONG A FRIEND?

FOR MORE THAN seventy years, the West has taken Turkey for granted. A staunch U.S. ally and member of NATO, Turkey is a strategic secular bridge between Europe and the Islamic East. But the days of such blissful complacency may now be over. Turkey's Welfare Party, which represents some of the extremes of Islamic fundamentalism, recently won the largest share of a parliamentary vote. While the vote was not strong enough to give the religious party control of the government, it is likely to leave Turkey in the hands of caretakers for the foreseeable future.

This next event didn't even make the newspapers. Turkey now has control over the headwaters of the Tigris and Euphrates rivers, making it possible for Istanbul to fulfill another biblical prophecy—shutting off the water flow to allow an invasion of the Middle East from Asia.

Revelation 16·12 should literally jump off the page when you ponder it: "And the sixth angel poured out his vial upon the great river Euphrates; and the water thereof was dried up, that the way of the kings of the east might be prepared."

Turkey is now in the final stages of building an agricultural-industrial project called the Southeast Anatolian Project, part of which involves controlling the rivers through large hydroelectric dams. This may be one of the most critical events taking place in the region.

## WHICH IS THE NEXT DOMINO?

INTERNAL AND external pressure for an Islamic state in Turkey is on the rise as the economy stumbles, and relations with the West are strained by Istanbul's incursion into Iraq against Kurdish rebels. Modern Turkey was founded on the ashes of the Ottoman Empire in 1923 by Mustafa Kemal Ataturk, who dreamed of a united secular state. The former leader may finally get his wish. Until recently, few questioned Ataturk's reforms. But as Turkey is spurned by Europe, it is being driven into the arms of Iran and other Islamic fundamentalist states. Even more significant is that it is drawing ever-closer in its relations to Russia.

This sets up the prophetic fulfillment of a last-days coalition of northern powers, including Togarmah (Turkey), that will invade Israel, as outlined in Ezekiel 38:2–6:

> "Son of man, set thy face against Gog, the land of Magog, the chief prince of Meshech and Tubal, and prophesy against him, And say, Thus saith the Lord GOD; Behold, I *am* against thee, O Gog, the chief prince of Meshech and Tubal: And I will turn thee back, and put hooks into thy jaws, and I will bring thee forth, and all thine army, horses and horsemen, all of them clothed with all sorts *of armour, even* a great company *with* bucklers and shields, all of them handling swords: Persia, Ethiopia, and Libya with them; all of them with shield and helmet: Gomer, and all his bands; the house of Togarmah (Turkey) of the north quarters, and all his bands: *and* many people with thee."

Like a lawyer who mounts evidence upon evidence, exhibit upon exhibit to prove his or her case, current events are coalescing, coming together to create a panorama of interrelated activity that literally shouts signs of the end.

Does it matter that Libya has accepted delivery of two SS-025 ballistic missiles capable of deploying nuclear warheads?

Does it matter that high-quality hundred-dollar bills made in Syria and Lebanon are flooding banks in Europe, the former Soviet Union, and the Far East? Intelligence officials believe the counterfeiters are trying to make a profit while destabilizing the U.S. economy.

> Libya has accepted delivery of two SS-025 ballistic missiles capable of deploying nuclear warheads.

Does it matter that Iran is expanding its five-billion-dollar quest for sophisticated weaponry to rebuild its arsenal, and that it recently attempted to strike a deal with South Africa for long-range artillery?

Does it matter that Iran's biological warfare has surged ahead with the help of the Russians? Intelligence reports indicate that the Iranians will move to a level of lethality that will be the equivalent of a nuclear weapon within a couple of years.

Does it matter that Iran, according to the best intelligence, will be able to build a nuclear weapon in less than three years?

Yes, it matters. It all matters greatly. Because each of these events is converging at the prophesied time—at the edge of eternity, the beginning of the new millennium, a period in the history of the world when nothing will ever be the same.

## IRAQ STILL BUILDING LONG-RANGE MISSILES

EVER A THREAT to Israel, Iraq is still attempting to build long-range ballistic missiles with the help of imports prohibited under United Nations sanctions. Investigators have concluded that an Iraq-bound shipment of sophisticated military equipment seized by Jordanian authorities was built in Russia, and may have been designed for use in intercontinental missiles. As Russia and China assist Iran in the development of nuclear weapons, the Iranian military is considering the strong possibility of an Israeli preemptive strike against its nuclear facilities.

**God's Word predicts what is now taking place.**

Ominously, an Iranian intelligence document has turned up in Israel, documenting that Tehran has retaliation plans in the event of such an attack. The scenario calls for a strike at Israel's own production and storage sites for nuclear weapons. In addition, Israeli targets around the world would be hit by terrorists.

Again, God's Word predicts what is now taking place. What clearer picture could one want than what is in Ezekiel 38:4–5: "And I will turn thee back, and put hooks into thy jaws, and I will bring thee forth, and all thine army, horses and horsemen, all of them clothed with all sorts *of armour, even* a great company *with* bucklers and shields, all of them handling swords: Persia, Ethiopia, and Libya with them; all of them with shield and helmet."

## TARGETING THE WEST

AMERICANS READ with amazement and growing concern that Nation of Islam leader Louis Farrakhan appeared in Libya with long-time America-hater Moammar Gadhafi. The purpose of their discussion was the role of American Muslims. To show how close the threat is coming to U.S. shores, the two militants discussed the formation of a Black Muslim lobby in the United States. It's now known that Gadhafi made good on his promise to send up to one billion dollars to help Farrakhan. This money was, at least in part, used to pay for the Million Man March in Washington D.C. Just weeks before the Farrakhan/ Gadhafi meeting, the Islamic Committee for the Defense of the Persecuted, a body close to the Mujahideen in Bosnia-Herzegovina, issued a terrorist threat to U.S. forces there.

But the threat is coming even closer to home. The United States has established a special thousand-man security unit on twenty-four-hour standby to deal exclusively with a nuclear terrorist attack. The Nuclear Emergency Search Team can reach any location in the country within four hours. To date, the group has been mobilized thirty times to deal with what turned out to be hoaxes in all cases. The group has been put on alert more than one hundred times, and believes that it is simply a matter of time before the United States is faced with a genuine nuclear terror attack.

## SCHOOL FOR TERRORISTS

HAVE YOU EVER wondered where international terrorists learn their trade? Now there's an answer. It's called the University of the Community of the Holy War, the nickname of the University of Dawat, and Jihad in Peshawar, Pakistan.

Pakistani officials are investigating the school's connections with terrorists in the Philippines, Central Asia, the Middle East, North Africa, and even those who plotted the World Trade Center bombing in New York City. U.S. investigators have cooperated with Pakistani intelligence services in their probe of the school.

Matthew 24:32 says, "Now learn a parable of the fig tree; When his branch is yet tender, and putteth forth leaves, ye know that summer *is* nigh."

Summer is nigh, indeed. The enemies of freedom and of the true God are studying books, field-testing weapons, creating havoc, and moving silently across international borders, seeking whom they may devour with their doctrine of hate.

The question is this: Are Christians studying as hard as the terrorists? Are believers spending as much time in God's Word as Islamic fundamentalists are poring over the words of their beloved Koran, a holy book that gives them their marching orders, their impetus, their motivation, and their reason for living? We are on a crash course with Islam, and the battle scene will not be pretty. The words of Genesis 6:11 are apropos: "The earth also was corrupt before God, and the earth was filled with violence."

"So shall it be at Christ's return" (Matthew 24:37).

## IRAQ'S CHEMICAL AND BIOLOGICAL ARMS

As IF THE possibility of terrorist training, espionage, and a proliferation of nuclear weapons were not sufficient to further destabilize the Middle East, new evidence suggests that Iraq withheld use of chemical weapons during the Persian Gulf War only because Saddam Hussein, who could easily have used its weapons of mass annihilation, simply chose not to. There is growing suspicion that the mysterious and varied symptoms of "Gulf War Syndrome," afflicting more than ten thousand veterans of the conflict, may be related to Iraq's biological warfare agents.

**Is "Gulf War Syndrome" related to Iraq's biological warfare agents?**

This should strike terror in the hearts of every mother and father in America who may at some future date see their sons or daughters sent to yet another conflict in that volatile region.

The news of these biological poisons still waiting to be used has even broader implications, based on the most recent intelligence findings. It's now reported that Saddam Hussein has been attempting to develop new biological weapons using ebola or similar viruses. According to reliable Russian sources, Iraq has already produced agents for rare and fatal African and Asian diseases. Other bio-weapons in Iraq's arsenal include botulinum and anthrax.

We've come a long way from *The Arabian Nights,* and the romanticization of life in the vast desert. This time, it's no fairy tale. Present leadership in the region is playing for keeps, and it's all part of the complex pattern of impending events that will eventually bring on the end.

## ARMAGEDDON COALITION FORMING

SYRIA, IRAN, AND TURKEY—three nations depicted in the Bible as forming an end-time coalition against Israel—have put their differences aside to establish themselves as a major regional power center. Here's where thoughtful people need to be aware: If Syrian President Hafaz Assad can manage to bring Iraq into this coalition—with or without Saddam Hussein—Western influence in the region will be thoroughly undermined.

Ezekiel 38:5 rings truer today than ever: "And I will fill his mountains with his slain men: in thy hills, and in thy valleys and in all thy rivers, shall they fall that are slain with the sword."

This is the Word of the Lord. The mountains will be filled with the dead; the valleys and rivers will contain the bodies of those defeated in battle. And the West will have little or no control—the region's power brokers know all too well how to maintain their stranglehold on their people and their land.

## QUESTIONS, BEWILDERMENT, TURMOIL?

AS WE HAVE looked into the pages of intelligence briefings that describe both the overt and covert activities of the Islamic states, we have been given a secular road map into the future. We've looked at facts, figures, military hardware, and weapons assessments. However, if this were all we had in our possession to assess the meaning of end-time events, it would be like trying to find a black cat in a dark room at midnight: hopeless. Fortunately, God has not left us in the dark. That's because the Bible is the ultimate roadmap that leads us to a deeper understanding of these alarming developments.

Ezekiel 38:8 describes modern-day Israel, after the Jews have returned from many nations and are apparently living securely in their new homeland. In search of safety for themselves and their families, the Jewish population of the former Soviet Union, Ethiopia, and Eastern Block nations has moved to Israel in record numbers. There they seem to be living more safely than ever before—especially following the "peace" agreements with Egypt, the PLO, and other Arab countries.

But the question remains: Are the current peace initiatives a prelude to that time of false peace so widely predicted in the Scriptures? No, we are not there yet, but the clock is ticking. Before peace comes, a strong European leader will emerge. He will seem to have the ultimate solution to the Middle East riddle. He will also reveal a means of implementing global government. It will be fascinating indeed to see how this "hero" relates to the world of Islam which, by that time, will have increased its political, military, and economic hold many times over.

The entire world will receive this man as the answer to its manifold problems. He will be a unifying figure of unprecedented appeal. At first, the world will be his dominion, and Israel will hardly be alone in placing itself in the hands of this benevolent European protectorate. But in so doing, Israelis will be signing a covenant with hell itself, through the person of the Antichrist, for he will betray Israel. We are told in Isaiah 28:15: "Because ye have said, We have made a covenant with death, and with hell are we at agreement; when the overflowing scourge shall pass through, it shall not come unto us: for we have made lies our refuge, and under false-hood have we hid ourselves."

> He will be a unifying figure of unprecedented appeal.

Ezekiel 38—a passage you will see often throughout this book—forecasts this period of false peace for the world—especially for the Jews. When they least expect trouble, God is going to cause the Russian leader (whomever Gog or Magog may be) to make a great tactical error. He is going to form a military alliance of Muslim nations against Israel, and launch a massive, blitzkrieg-like attack. As a result, the entire world will be engulfed in the greatest holocaust in history.

How is the alliance of Muslim nations going to have the power to do this? Right now they are positioning themselves politically, economically, and militarily throughout the region. This ongoing preparation, coupled with an ever-increasing spate of terrorist activity, will continue to destabilize, threaten, and keep the West on red alert.

The Bible tells us that there will be an alliance of Arab, African, and Islamic nations united with the Republic of Russia. And, as we have seen, Russia is being linked more and more closely to this emerging new Islamic world order. According to Scripture, Russia will seem to blunder its way into mankind's final war as if acting against its own will. In the light of its unholy alliance, it's interesting to note the way, even today, the Islamic world defers to Russia, overlooking offenses while holding other international powers—especially the United States—to a much higher standard of international behavior.

## TURNING A BLIND EYE

ONE EXAMPLE is the deafening silence from Islamic nations

concerning Russia's invasion of Chechnya—a mostly Muslim republic. Where were the outcries, the righteous indignation, the murderous wails and screams for justice for "our Chechan brothers and sisters"? None came from the Islamic world. Why?

And why do you suppose that after the breakup of the U.S.S.R., Iran decided not to recognize any of the former Soviet republics as independent Islamic states, preferring instead to allow them closer linkage to Russia and the C.I.S. (Commonwealth of Independent States). Individually, those Asian Islamic nations would have little political influence over Moscow. But together they have great power and influence over the leaders in the Russian capital. I can assure you that right now Iran is anticipating that time when the Islamic world can draw Russia, along with its Islamic satellite nations, into an alliance against Israel.

## ON THE EDGE OF ETERNITY

WE HAVE TALKED at some length about the threat of Islam, and how militant Islamic fundamentalists will continue to make our world an increasingly dangerous place for all. That's why I urge you to read the daily papers with even greater wisdom, awareness, and understanding. Look for the subtleties in press reports. Read your Bible with fresh eyes, and with a view to developing a deeper understanding of end-time prophecies.

And while current events in the Middle East are critical pieces in the end-time puzzle, there is also a parade of other circumstances that will fill out the requirements for millennial activity. We know, for example, that the secular world paints a picture of great international angst as we approach the year 2000. Forced smiles hide the true fears of millions. Economic chaos and moral bankruptcy are the orders of the day.

Meanwhile, the church is also grappling with the meaning of the millennium. Some are even fearful that the world is coming to an end. Unfortunately, a degree in biblical illiteracy has been granted to too many as a surprising number of Christians associate the end with the return of Jesus Christ to earth. Such is not the case.

Are we approaching the close of the age? Yes, the clock of time inexorably ticks on. Is there really gloom and doom on the horizon? Most assuredly, and there will be more. In fact, no other period in human history has witnessed so many threats to the survival of the human race. Never before has the stage been so well set for Christ's Second Coming. The geopolitical alliances have been forged. The climactic conditions are in evidence. The spiritual status of the world is about what we would expect. Think about our world today:

- Major Christian denominations have been captured by those who reject the essential truth of the Bible, and the deity of Jesus Christ (2 Peter 2:1–2).

- Bible-believing Christians are openly persecuted for their beliefs—by governments, by other religious leaders, sometimes even by so-called ministers of the gospel (John 16:2).

- There is widespread—even rampant—interest in and acceptance of Eastern religions, extrasensory perception, astrology, witchcraft, and false prophets (1 Timothy 4:1; Revelation 9:20).

- We see a serious movement toward a one-world religion system, with Pope John Paul II himself fearing the rise of the antichrist and an "anti-Pope" in the near future (Revelation 13:1, 11, and 17:9).

- The site of the Temple in Jerusalem is so important to the two faiths that it may well be the most controversial, explosive piece of land on the face of the earth—and one of the key pieces of the end-time puzzle. Israelis talk openly about the importance of rebuilding the Temple in Jerusalem. Jewish law demands that the Temple be rebuilt on the very sight of its earlier ruins. Unfortunately, the future Temple site is currently the location of two of Islam's holiest shrines—the Dome of the Rock, and the Al Aqsa Mosque. This places the Jews and those of the Islamic faith on a collision course. Nonetheless, the Temple *will* be rebuilt, and it will be the prelude to the climax of history (Ezekiel chapters 40–48).

- The Middle East—particularly the rampages of a radical, fundamentalist Islam—remains a constant source of tension, and a flashpoint for a future world war (Ezekiel 38:1, 2, 15, 16).

- The United States is abdicating its preeminent leadership position in the world in favor of multilateralism, globalism, and interdependence (Revelation 13:7).

- Europe is increasingly moving toward unification, and the rest of the world is forming regional military and economic alliances that will make eventual global convergence inevitable (Daniel 7:8, 20, 23, 24).

- As never before, people throughout the world are yearning for a leader to bring them together (Daniel 11:36).

- The worst famines the world has ever known are breaking out (Revelation 6:5, 6).

- New epidemics of old plagues are spreading, and new diseases are ravaging the planet, even as modern medicine and technology should be overcoming such maladies (Luke 21:11).

- Moral chaos in America is tearing apart the fabric of our society—with no end in sight. (Revelation 9:21).

- Drug addiction, physical, emotional, and sexual abuse are becoming enemies in America, and throughout the world—West and East (Revelation 18:23).

- Crime, riots, unemployment, poverty, illiteracy, mental illness, illegitimacy, and other social problems are also on the rampage (Matthew 24:12).

After we have factored in all this human conflict, it's important to remember Jesus promised that the generation witnessing the return of Jerusalem into Jewish custody would not pass until "all these things" be fulfilled, including the return of the King (Luke 21:24).

Jesus is not coming to destroy the world. He's coming to *save* it, to *rebuild it,* to *give it hope.* That's what Revelation 11:18 and Matthew 19:28 are all about. Those who link the physical return of Jesus with the end of the world are, charitably speaking, committing a grievous scriptural error.

As we come to the end of this chapter, may I say something clearly, forcefully, and yet in Christian love? The world is not coming to an end—not now, not in the year 2000, and not even after the thousand-year reign over the world by Jesus Himself. On the contrary, the Bible—both Old and New Testaments— is unequivocal in stating that the world will never end. (See Isaiah 45:17; Ecclesiastes 1:4; Psalm 104:5; Ephesians 3:21; Hebrews 1:8.)

God's will is going to be done on earth as it is in heaven. There will be a period of time in the future in which this is so. It hasn't happened yet, but it's coming. The only questions are when, and for how long.

> God's will is going to be done on earth as it is in heaven.

We know it's going to take more than an "Open Sesame," as spoken by Ali Baba, to open ourselves to a full understanding of the end times. Christians need to think, pray, read, study, and ask the Holy Spirit for discernment in knowing how to interpret what are so often bewildering and disturbing events. Rejoice that our God is a God of understanding, insight, and wisdom, all of which He freely shares with you and me.

## THIS NEWS FLASH JUST IN . . .

### 19 KILLED, 10 INJURED IN

### JERUSALEM BUS EXPLOSION

As I was reading this Reuters news report, as is the case with so many of these news flashes, it sickened me. It read,

"A bomb exploded aboard a bus in the heart of Jerusalem today, killing at least nineteen people, including the bomber, and injuring a dozen others, according to Israeli police. The blast occurred almost exactly one week after an Islamic suicide bomber killed twenty-five people in a similar attack on the same bus line. The Islamic militant group Hamas has claimed responsibility for the latest blast, as it did two bombings last week. Hamas said today's attack ends its revenge for the slaying of its master bombmaker Yahya Ayyash, 'The Engineer,' and it says it is giving Israel three months to respond to an offer of a truce.

"Palestinian President Yasser Arafat acted swiftly to meet Israeli demands for tough security measures today, by outlawing the military wings of the Hamas and Islamic Jihad organizations in the Palestinian self-rule areas of the West Bank and Gaza Strip. But in Damascus, a spokesman for the Popular Front for the Liberation of Palestine warned that any steps by Arafat to crack down on militant activity in the self-rule areas would only result in more violence. He said the attacks will continue 'and neither Arafat nor Israel will be able to stop them.'"

The report continued . . .

"Crowds, allowed nearer the cleared scene, roared: 'Death to the Arabs,' 'Revenge, revenge' and, in a reference to the assassination of Prime Minister Yitzhak Rabin on November 4 by a right-wing Jew: 'Peres is next in line.'

"In schools throughout Israel, parties celebrating Purim—a holiday marking the salvation of Jews from genocide in ancient Persia—were canceled. Children, costumed for parties, instead gathered around their teachers and televisions to talk about Sunday's horror."

The June 1996 terrorist bombing in Saudi Arabia that killed nineteen Americans and wounded hundreds of others is further evidence of the escalating violence. The region is about to boil over.

When will it end? When will there be peace? Not now, and not in the near future. That seems to be a promise of the Islamic militants to the Jewish people. Sadly, this news report adds to factual reports we've been discussing in this chapter. In Hebrew, Jerusalem means "city of peace," but the truth is that holy place has been—and is even now—a place of fear, war, and wanton destruction.

Students of Scripture will not be surprised, however, because they remember that real peace

> Jerusalem means "city of peace". . . .

can only come when the Prince of Peace returns. Until then, there will be no lasting peace on earth. And the ever-increasing crescendo of "peace rhetoric" that has already begun is but a another sign of impending end-time destruction. Ironically, it is the harbinger of history's bloodiest hour—the Time of Jacob's Trouble. (See Jeremiah 30:4; Daniel 12:1; Matthew 24:21; Revelation 7:14.)

As we continue to view the unraveling of history in the volatile Middle East, we can only pray that God gives us keen eyes, discerning minds, and hearts of understanding so that we may be able to understand the times in which we live. We will especially need God-given insight and knowledge as we now grapple with yet another issue of great end-time importance—the inevitable coming world government. That influential, international, highly-regarded globalist movement the Bible prophesies will come to pass just before Jesus returns to earth (2 Thessalonians 2:3–8).

## 5

## THE COMING
## ONE-WORLD GOVERNMENT

Let me see your papers." Those five heart-stopping words, spoken by unsmiling border guards or Gestapo-style soldiers, have struck terror in the hearts of millions of people throughout our century. They have been—and still are—the words of the police state, the words of military bullies young and old who have been granted the authority to intimidate, torture, and kill. But now, with the advent of surveillance technology and other scientific breakthroughs, super computers are bringing us ever closer to the day when identification papers will no longer be necessary. In the future, the "papers" will be tiny microchips, and they'll be more effective than any document ever scrutinized at a border crossing.

### A "Miniature" Big Brother

One day soon, the experts tell us, men and women worldwide may be required to receive a biochip implant in the hand or head that will limit their ability to buy and sell, travel, and work. Terry Cook, an expert who has studied developments in such "biometric" devices, states:

> "We are getting closer all the time to that day when biochip implants will be used on human beings. Hitler's Third Reich demanded that all German citizens had to carry identification and could be stopped at any time by either civilian or military people. The day may not be far off when we can be stopped at any time and have scanners waved over us as we approach the final states of the biochip and ID technology of the New World Order system."

The biochips necessary for such a "Big-Brother-is-watching" program have actually been around for more than a decade. The technology is already in full use in several U.S. cities and counties in animal control work. Animal shelters and clinics are clamoring for an ID system that will link all government animal regulation and control agencies, pounds, and veterinarians throughout the country. Not surprisingly, the cheerleaders of one-world government have also been quick to champion such a system for human beings.

**Will the U.S. government jump on the biochip bandwagon?**

"The technology behind such a microchip is fairly uncomplicated, and with a little refinement could be used in a variety of human applications," explains Tim Willard, executive officer of the World Future Society. Willard continues, "Conceivably, a number could be assigned at birth and go with a person throughout life. At the checkout stand at the supermarket, you would simply pass your hand over a scanner and your bank account would automatically be debited."

Will the U.S. government jump on the biochip bandwagon? Americans remain inherently skeptical about such a "Big Brother" arrangement. But it may not be long before the power brokers in Washington take a more serious look at this opportunity to exercise virtually global control over its citizens.

In the meantime, to promote "national identification" as a top priority, there must be the perception of need—some crisis to be solved.

## REPUBLICANS AND DEMOCRATS AGREEING ON SOMETHING?

THE GOLDEN STATE of California, in the eyes of some, has lost its glitter. This is due in large part to the economic pain of unauthorized border crossings from Mexico, and the need for unprecedented economic support of illegals. In this situation, the probability of a biochip is enjoying increasing popularity. Democrats such as Senator Dianne Feinstein and Republicans like Governor Pete Wilson agree the time has come for a national identity card, perhaps including biometric data. Such a card is already in use by the federal government.

To the student of biblical prophecy, the name of the card should arouse considerable interest: The device is called MARC, and stands for "Multi-technology Automated Reader Card." The MARC is currently being used in the military and can be readied for virtually any other form of information retrieval.

Feinstein has called on her colleagues in the U.S. Congress to make carrying such a card mandatory for every American citizen. Her remarks, memorialized in the *Daily Washington Journal Roll Call,* are chilling in their content:

"I believe that a new, phone- or machine-readable card that all job benefits applicants would be required to present to verify their work or eligibility for assistance deserves careful consideration. As (the Senate Subcommittee on Immigration) heard (from representatives of the State Department, INS, FBI, Social Security Administration, Secret Service, state and motor vehicle authorities), counterfeit-resistant cards that incorporate 'biometric' data are available and in use today. Whether the card carries a magnetic strip on which the bearer's unique voice, retina pattern, or fingerprint is digitally encoded, or whether it incorporates a digitized photo and signature integrated into the plastic card itself, it is clear to me that state-of-the-art work and benefits eligibility IDs can and must replace the Dinosaur Age documents now being used."

## Danger Ahead

FEINSTEIN HAS URGED Congress not to wait—but to act immediately to begin creating such a system. Fortunately, some opposition has arisen to thwart the senator's plans. Still, the vast majority of Americans are blissfully unaware that such dangerous designs are even being considered in the hallowed halls of Congress.

A computer software entrepreneur has observed that a national ID database threatens civil liberty. A system employing tens of thousands of government clerks and administrators, and costing tens of billions of dollars to build and operate, would surely soon be expanded beyond such benign uses as child-tracking. The expert muses:

"Why not use it, at virtually no additional cost, to track convicted child molesters as well? Who would dare object? Why not then also track the movements of convicts and murderers? And rapists. And drug dealers, and felons in general. And fathers behind in child support. And tax-evaders. And 'political extremists.' Members of 'religious cults.' Drug addicts. AIDS carriers. Gun owners. Each turn of the political cycle, left and right would add their favorite batch of social enemies to the surveillance list."

## Is the Biochip the "Mark?"

WHAT DOES God's Word say about the scenarios being floated in America's corridors of power? Could information embedded in tiny biochips be the personal end-time ID code we are warned of in the Bible? Scripture tells us that in the future, a one-world system of government will require every person to receive a "mark" in his or her right hand or in their foreheads. Without this "mark of the beast," no one will be permitted to buy or sell. In years past, few could envision such a system in operation. The technology simply did not exist. But today, with what amounts to virtually daily breakthroughs in biometric technology, these advances now make such a system not only viable, but plausible. Is there any doubt that we are now a few miles further down the road toward a Big Brother-style global dictatorship?

> Revelation 13:16–18 reminds us, "And he causeth all, both small and great, rich and poor, free and bond, to receive a mark in their right hand, or in their foreheads: And that no man might buy or sell, save he that had the mark, or the name of the beast, or the number of his name. Here is wisdom. Let him that hath understanding count the number of the beast: for it is the number of a man; and his number is Six hundred threescore *and* six."

## ANTI-FAMILY CRUSADE

WHILE THE "MARK" will be individualized, "group think" will become universal in the last days. One attempt at such community thinking took place in September 1995, when delegates from one hundred seventy nations attended the United Nations Fourth World Conference on Women in Beijing, China. Prior to the event, Dr. James Dobson warned, "It will be the most radical, atheistic, and anti-family crusade in the history of the world, and your government is pulling the strings and will support a disproportionate share of the costs."

Concerned Christians should be grateful to Dr. Dobson for his red-flag warnings about the now-historic festival for militant feminists, women adamant about imposing their radical beliefs on the entire world. While in Beijing these women were surely not thinking of the end times, nor were they even remotely aware that they'd become pawns of history in the making. Yet their clearly abrasive goals should remind Christians that what they have proposed falls directly into the one-world-order file. While the conference is now history, its international effect lingers on, as the conferees continue to support their objectives, three of which are:

- *The elimination of marriage:* Feminists consider this to be the root of all evil, and blame the family for violence against women.

- *The promotion of "gender feminism":* This new approach to human sexuality encourages the notion that the biological differences between men and women are relatively insignificant—thus, the traditional roles of mother and father should be abandoned.

- *The politicization of speech:* They want to eliminate the use of ordinary words such as "wife," "husband," "son," "daughter," "brother," "sister," and "manhood" because these terms are "sexist."

With all its timeless, ancient traditions of science, philosophy, and culture, China remains a nation that holds the record for the abuse and oppression of women, which made the conference—held on China's soil—yet one more cruel irony. China's forced-abortion policies, and its one-child-per-family law make women not only state prisoners of government-imposed restrictions, but also so much chattel for what has historically remained a male-dominated society.

As he continues to sensitize the world to Chinese abuses of women and children, Dobson continues, "This [China] is a nation that monitors menstrual cycles so it can identify young women with unapproved pregnancies and drag them into medical clinics to have their babies killed. It is also a country that has murdered tens of millions of female infants. So effective has been its bias against the feminine gender, that the sex-ratio in large regions of China favors males by 64 percent. What irony, then, that the people who have annihilated their little girls will host a conference on the betterment of women. What breathtaking wickedness."

Yet, the beat goes on in the world's highest echelons of power. Headlines promise a new age: "The best is yet before us," declare those who have no understanding of the times. "We are on the edge of human breakthroughs that will bring our world together in peace and brotherhood," rhapsodize others. Even the officials of the world's largest "talk shop" are declaring their careless optimism for the future.

## UN OFFICIAL ON THE "MILLENNIUM"

"IN MY VIEW, from all perspectives—scientific, political, social, economic, and ideological—humanity finds itself in the pregnancy of an entirely new and promising age: the global, interdependent, universal age. . . . the birth of the global brain, heart, senses, and soul to humanity, of a holistic consciousness of our place in the universe and on this planet, and of our role and destiny in them." Those are the words of former United Nations Assistant Secretary General Robert Muller in his article, "Preparing for the Next Millennium."

> What does God's Word say about the coming world government?

But Muller doesn't stop there. He continues, "We must, together, create an agency within the UN and perhaps an independent united religious secretariat. What an incredible challenge that would offer to the United Nations, and what untold good it would bring to humanity, which desperately needs a moral and spiritual Renaissance."

I could not agree with Muller more on his last sentence—that we need a "moral and spiritual Renaissance." Muller and I quickly part company, however, when he suggests this great inner personal reform be accomplished under the aegis of a morally bankrupt United Nations, a body that not only possesses limited real power, but what power it has, remains questionable to its core.

What does God's Word say about the coming world government and the growing international movement that promises a "moral and spiritual Renaissance" to all who will jump on board? There are two passages that display the counsel of Scripture, from the books of Daniel and Matthew. Hear the Word of the Lord:

> "And he shall speak *great* words against the most High, and shall wear out the saints of the most High, and think to change times and laws: and they shall be given into his hand until a time and times and the dividing of time. But the judgment shall sit, and they shall take away his dominion, to consume and to destroy *it* unto the end. And the kingdom and dominion, and the greatness of the kingdom under the whole heaven, shall be given to the people of the saints of the most High, whose kingdom *is* an everlasting kingdom, and all dominions shall serve and obey him."
>
> —DANIEL 7:25–27

> "All these *are* the beginning of sorrows. Then shall they deliver you up to be afflicted, and shall kill you: and ye shall be hated of all nations for my name's sake. And then shall many be offended, and shall betray one another, and shall hate one another. And many false prophets shall rise, and shall deceive many."
>
> —MATTHEW 24:8–11 (SEE ALSO REVELATION 13:7, 8.)

## DECEIVERS OF MANKIND

WHAT WILL THESE false prophets of the end time look like? How will they be recognized? How will their thinking contribute to a "one-mind" government? Will these individuals be cleverly disguised? Or will they ply their wickedness openly?

Let's look at some of these false prophets of the millennium, who further confirm that earth's final hour quickly approaches the stroke of midnight.

## CENTRAL ASIA'S NEW SEER

A NEW "PROPHET" has emerged in Central Asia. His name is Akbeket Sufihan, and he bills himself as the last messenger from God. Sufihan's new book, *Allah's New Greeting to the World,* is attracting the attention of the Islamic world—as well as Russians who are alarmed about religious agitation in this strategic area.

## MESSAGES FROM BEYOND THE GRAVE

OUIJA BOARDS are apparently out as a way to connect with the long-departed in this age of computers and cyberspace. According to a new book, *Conversations Beyond the Light,* the dead are more likely to communicate with the living by E-mail, fax, modems, or phone calls.

Authors Pat Kubis and Mark Macy believe the dead are sending messages from the planet Marduk, in the Spiral Galaxy NGC4866 on the third astral plane. Marduk reportedly has three suns, skyscrapers, blimps, and a river that encircles the globe. Its inhabitants, according to Kubis, include Eleanor Roosevelt, giants, Indians living in teepees, cavemen, and Vikings. Before we disregard as foolishness these wild wizards of deceit, we must remember that tens of thousands of men, women, and children throughout the world are being duped into believing their lies. It is a sign of the times.

## WORLD RELIGIONS TALK OF UNITING

IN A FURTHER bid to bring the world to one point of view, there is now a movement afoot to establish a permanent

"United Religions" (UR) organization. A charter setting up the UN-style group is currently being drafted, and a facility to promote this point of view may well be open in the near future. Like the UN, the UR will have a five-hundred-member assembly, a thirty-six-member executive council, and a secretary general. Comprised of representatives of religions both large and small, the group would meet once or twice a year to "reverse the use of religion to justify war, hate, violence, aggression, and intolerance." Peacemaker Teams of spiritual leaders and conflict-resolution specialists would be dispatched to trouble spots throughout the world. The origins of UR—perhaps the predecessor to the global church prophesied in the Bible—are in the World Parliament of Religions, which has already convened to adopt "a new world ethic."

## No-Fault Adultery

Backing up the call of the Anglican Bishop of Edinburgh in Scotland to stop condemning adultery, a Church of England release says that the phrase "living in sin" should no longer be used. The report also urged a "ready welcome" for practicing homosexuals in the church. The Archbishop of Canterbury, George Carey, leader of the Church of England, welcomed the report as a "rich resource in a continuing process of debate and soul-searching."

## Japan's Poison Gas Cult

If people believe that Aum Shinrikyo, the Japanese cult suspected of the March 1995 subway gas attacks in Tokyo, was only a regional threat, they need to guess again. The sect, with some 10,000 followers in Japan and 30,000 in Russia, was working actively to bring about global disaster and warfare by 1997. There is evidence they had the potential to do just that. The group's chemical production facilities were, according to investigators, "larger, more sophisticated, and of better quality than Iraq's chemical gas plants, and are good enough to produce highly purified sarin." The sect has also made efforts to establish links to the Russian military and recruit chemical and biological warfare experts into its ranks.

Shoko Asahara, the group's leader who has proclaimed himself the second coming of Christ, reportedly hopes to create enough disorder, death, and mayhem worldwide to attract masses to his cult as earth's only remaining safe haven, thus building Aum Shinrikyo into a universal religion.

> ". . . in the latter times some shall depart from the faith, giving heed to seducing spirits. . . ."

As I read this report, my mind went immediately to three passages of Scripture. First Timothy 4:1–2 says, "Now the Spirit speaketh expressly, that in the latter times some shall depart from the faith, giving heed to seducing spirits, and doctrines of devils; Speaking lies in hypocrisy; having their conscience seared with a hot iron."

Revelation 9:20, 21 reminds us, "And the rest of the men which were not killed by these plagues yet repented not of the works of their hands, that they should not worship devils, and idols of gold, and silver, and brass, and stone, and of wood: which neither can see, nor hear, nor walk: Neither repented they of their murders, nor of their sorceries, nor of their fornication, nor of their thefts."

Luke 21:7–11 says, "And they asked him, saying, Master, but when shall these things be? and what sign *will there be* when these things shall come to pass? And he said, Take heed that ye be not deceived: for many shall come in my name, saying, I am *Christ;* and the time draweth near: go ye not therefore after them. But when ye shall hear of wars and commotions, be not terrified: for these things must first come to pass; but the end *is* not by and by. Then said he unto them, Nation shall rise against nation, and kingdom against kingdom: And great earthquakes shall be in divers places, and famines, and pestilences; and fearful sights and great signs shall there be from heaven."

## Brazen Discussions of One-world Government

FEARFUL SIGHTS and great signs, indeed! One is former Soviet dictator Mikhail Gorbachev's personal blueprint for global government. Crediting himself with having ended the cold war, the Russian leader took it upon himself to convene a five-day meeting in San Francisco of world and political leaders who openly discussed the need for one-world government, and the establishment of a new morality free of the constraints of Christian values.

Numerous heads of state participated—former leaders such as former President George Bush, and ex-Prime Minister Margaret Thatcher, media titans ranging from Ted Turner to Ted Koppel, and an eclectic collection of personalities including General Colin Powell, filmmaker Oliver Stone, and singer John Denver. However, a virtual press blackout ensured that many of the details of the "State of the World Forum" remain unpublished.

We do know Gorbachev's "wish list":

- Further negotiated arms cuts.

- Move toward more regional networks—such as NAFTA.

- Expanded membership in the United Nations Security Council.

- Dismantling of all nuclear warheads.

And we also know this about the conference: much of its information plays into the context of end-time prophesies. As we scrambled for these documents, we learned that Gorbachev's meeting to convey his blueprint for global government was only one of five annual conferences scheduled to foster global "independence" and eventually deal a death blow to national sovereignty. The meeting promised to continue to demand action on the following issues:

- A supra-national authority must quickly take charge of the world's arsenal of nuclear weapons, environmental policies, and distribution of wealth and resources.

- The world of interdependence and cooperation must absolutely rule out the use of force, particularly of nuclear weapons, as the solution to any problems.

- There must be a push for honoring diversity, and honoring the earth. It is this combination that will create the basis for worldwide unity.

- There must be a new form of global socialism—the only acceptable road to this New World Order.

In Gorbachev's book, *The Search for a New Beginning: Developing a New Civilization,* published for the conference, there is a denouncement of nationalism, inequitable distribution of resources, and development that takes a toll on the environment and weapons spending and research. "The time has come to develop integrated global policies," writes the former Russian leader. "This need is all the greater since the obvious crisis of the entire system of international relations is just one of the manifestations of the malaise of our civilization."

Some 275 of the 500 participants paid $5,000 apiece to rub shoulders with people such as Jane Fonda, Carl Sagan, Nelson Mandela, Mario Cuomo, and Bill Gates. Except for South Africa's Desmond Tutu, Christian leaders were uniformly excluded from the meeting.

> Some 275 of the 500 participants paid $5,000 apiece to rub shoulders with people such as Jane Fonda, Carl Sagan, Nelson Mandela, Mario Cuomo, and Bill Gates.

Was this conference—and the series of scheduled follow-up meetings—a mere blip on the end-time screen? Will these New Age, pantheistic get-togethers ultimately be of relative unimportance? Or might they be harbingers of what to expect from other world leaders in other places as we approach the end? In the days just before Jesus returns to earth, Scripture portrays a world governed not only by a central authority, but by a global religious entity as well. Clearly, the premillennial convergence of such prestigious and influential political, cultural, and "spiritual leaders" at Gorbachev's behest is significant.

As our final arbiter of Truth, we again look at the Word of God for the answers to the end-time puzzle. "Then if any man shall say unto you, Lo, here *is* Christ, or there; believe *it* not. For there shall arise false Christs, and false prophets, and shall show great signs and wonders; insomuch that, *if it were* possible, they shall deceive the very elect" (Matthew 24:23–24).

"And I stood upon the sand of the sea, and saw a beast rise up out of the sea, having seven heads and ten horns, and upon his horns ten crowns, and upon his heads the name of blasphemy. And the beast which I saw was like unto a leopard, and his feet were as *the feet* of a bear, and his mouth as the mouth of a lion: and the dragon gave him his power, and his seat, and great authority. And I saw one of his heads as it were wounded to death; and his deadly wound was healed: and all the world wondered after the beast. And they worshipped the dragon which gave power unto the beast: and they worshipped the beast, saying, Who *is* like unto the beast? who is able to make war with him? And there was given unto him a mouth speaking great things and blasphemies; and power was given unto him to continue forty *and* two months. And he opened his mouth in blasphemy against God, to blaspheme his name, and his tabernacle, and them that dwell in heaven. And it was given unto him to make war with the saints, and to overcome them: and power was given him over all kindreds, and tongues, and nations" (Revelation 13:1–7).

## UNITED NATIONS: GLOBAL REVENUE SERVICE

WHAT BETTER WAY for a "Big Brother" organization to "overcome the saints" than through a merciless form of taxation? It's now official. A United Nations agency is openly advocating the need for a one-world government and global taxation. This declaration by the UN Development Program came to light during the recent World Summit for Social Development in Denmark.

Here's what Nobel Prize-winning economist Jan Tinbregen said about the need for a "global human security fund."

> "Mankind's problems can no longer be solved by national governments. What is needed is a world government. This can best be achieved by strengthening the United Nations system."

What an incredible comment! But the UN is not alone. While the United Nations may be spearheading this globalist movement, there are many other organizations now openly working on behalf of a one-world order—the kind prophesied in the Bible for the days just before Jesus returns to earth. Here are four examples of such groups active in one-worldism:

- *The World Constitution and Parliament Association* in Colorado has been taking out advertisements in newspapers around the country, promoting the idea of one-world government. It proposes placing the oceans, seabeds, Antarctica, and even the moon under the protectorate of a Federal World Government. The group continues to hold international meetings to declare its laws in "full force and effect." Whether or not this association succeeds in its objectives, the very idea that it is already so active—and attracting so many adherents—is a reminder that such a movement is yet another sign of the times.

- *Warstop!* This is another group that uses newspaper ads to "make enforced global law the primary aim of American foreign policy." Warstop! is also working in schools and with political candidates to further its international agenda.

- *Philadelphia II* is placing voter initiatives to create world government on state ballots. Movements are currently active in California, Kansas, Illinois, and Missouri. Former U.S. Senator Mike Gravel of Alaska is a principal proponent of this approach, which seeks to convene a World Constitutional Convention.

- *A New Age religious group* with connections to the Maharishi Mahesh Yogi is pushing to make Israel the capital of "One Government for One World." The Jewish activists behind this idea promise that the meditation techniques offered by the Maharishi will unleash psychic powers that will not only make the Jewish state independent, but will be a great spiritual resource to the entire world. Daniel 7:23 states, "Thus he said, The fourth beast shall be the fourth kingdom upon earth, which shall be diverse from all kingdoms, and shall devour the whole earth, and shall tread it down, and break it in pieces." The phrase "shall be diverse from all kingdoms" is the key phrase in this prophecy.

The idea of a one-world government is not isolated to the West or the East. It is a disparate movement that is evolving independently from various international ideological sources. This erroneous thinking is coming from "diverse kingdoms" of the world. But the snowball is gathering momentum.

Even though these organizations may be small and lacking in influence at this time, their aggregate power will only increase as we edge closer to the year 2000 and the beginning of the millennium. On the surface, for many, these movements that "bring us all together" may seem plausible, logical, and even life-sustaining. Therefore the question: Does each of these movements, small or large, in fact, lay one more brick in the groundwork of a one-world political and economic system, as the Bible portrays for the planet in the last days? Hal Lindsey reminds us, "When you get beyond the lofty rhetoric and analyze just what is meant by global government, the reality can be even more frightening than the instability of a hostile world governed by the aggressive use of force." The concept of one-world government is the only way to "save" the world in the minds of many. Without global participation by informed, enthusiastic, albeit scattered entities, our planet has no hope, it is alleged.

> Promis is a computer program with enormous "snooping" powers.

But to foster that hope, increased surveillance must be the order of the day. Enter "Promis."

## THE PROMIS AND THE OCTOPUS

IT'S STILL TRUE: big, influential, earth-shaking things can— and often do—come in small packages. Here's yet another example. Back in the 1980s, a small computer software company, Inslaw, developed a program called Promis. Originally designed exclusively to track court cases, it was soon discovered that Promis had far-reaching applications in the fields of finance and global intelligence.

Because of Promis' much anticipated "promise" in the vast areas of surveillance, it was awarded a contract with the Justice Department. But, as federal court records and two congressional investigations reveal, U.S. government officials replicated the Promis software and left Inslaw in bankruptcy court.

Now, sources within Inslaw suggest that the pirated versions of the Promis software contain a "trap door" that gives the National Security Agency and other intelligence operations enormous "snooping" powers. With this tool at their disposal, these government-sponsored groups now have the capability to monitor the computers of foreign banks and security agencies to track wire transfers, and invade even the most secure data storage systems in the world.

## A Journalist Disappears

A BOOK RECENTLY released, *The Internet Insider* by Ruffin Prevost, indicates that Promis is being used to compile a so-called "doomsday" data file. Several years ago, Danny Cassalario, a brave young investigative reporter, began his own inquiry into the Inslaw case. He told friends he was about to reveal some astonishing details in a story titled "The Octopus." Only days away from completing his story, Cassalario was found dead, his notes missing.

Again, the question: Could it be that this labyrinthine system of one-world ideas will continue to converge to lay the foundation for a one-world economic and political framework just as the Bible prophesies for the end of the world as we know it?

I would suggest that the answer is an unequivocal *yes*, and that it will only need a major economic crisis to spark global controls.

## The Coming World Economic Disaster

ECONOMISTS THE WORLD over are scrambling to revise their global financial forecasts in light of many discouraging factors—not the least of which is an epidemic of negligence and poor judgment by some of the world's leading politicians. What I'm about to write should not be taken in a partisan manner, but must be viewed as a matter of record. Because without a foundation of solid understanding, our house will become a house of cards indeed.

Unfortunately, some of that poor judgment has been initiated in our own White House. President Clinton, for instance, gives lip service to balancing the budget and controlling the sky-rocketing growth of government spending, but he says he will veto a congressional plan that would actually accomplish those goals with a modest cut of only 1 percent. The president says that's too much reduction. It's inhuman. It will cause too much pain, too much suffering. The truth is that to continue the pattern of irresponsible spending will bring on far more pain and suffering than the modest and sensible cuts being proposed.

## WHERE ARE THE COURAGEOUS?

FURTHER, BOTH POLITICAL parties in the United States have shown a stunning lack of courage in dealing with the coming Social Security crash. In 1950, sixteen workers contributed to the system for every one recipient. Today, that ratio has shrunk to three-to-one, and within thirty years, it will fall to two-to-one. Economists now estimate that a lifetime tax rate of a confiscatory 84 percent will soon be needed to sustain the growth of Social Security spending.

But President Clinton is just one of many key world leaders who seems to believe there is no limit to how heavily taxes can be piled on the backs of ordinary people to pay for government excess.

## ECONOMIC DISASTER LOOMING IN EUROPE AND ASIA

EVEN THE AVOWEDLY conservative British government keeps heaping more financial burden on its people, leaving consumers in that island nation with less and less to spend in an already down-sized economy. France, too, is following the socialist path. Its new prime minister, Alain Juppe, has championed a policy that will soon raise the minimum wage above its current level of U.S. $12,000—a benchmark that is already killing hundreds of thousands of jobs, and strangling the most productive segment of the population.

In Germany, where the Deutschmark has long served as a source of national pride, leaders in Bonn are preparing to abandon one of the world's most stable currencies in favor of a new, standardized European currency. Many average Germans are asking, "Why?" Why, since the current European currency, the ECU, has depreciated 40 percent against the Deutschmark?

In Japan, an elite bureaucracy runs a command-and-control economy in combination with leading cartels. The tight regulations imposed from the top keep prices high, and make undeniably poor use of the nation's resources. In addition, Japan's well-known policies of protectionism are stifling free trade the world over.

## COULD IT GET ANY WORSE?

JUST HOW BAD is the world economy getting? Coutts & Company, the English "bank to the elite," painted a bleak—but what I consider to be a realistic, truthful—picture of the global economy in one of its recent issues of *International Investment Review*. This is not hype. These are the words of a conservative English banking house: "In the United States, there is a stalemate between the president and Congress; in Italy, the government teeters on the brink of chaos. In France, Spain, and Belgium . . . [there are] various scandals; China and Thailand face a time of uncertainty with the probable demise of venerable rulers. The situation in the area of the former Soviet Union remains disturbingly unsettled. Africa looks set for mass genocide."

**We are sitting naively on an economic powder keg.**

Not a happy report, but I'm confident that since you read your daily newspaper and watch the news on television, such an account comes as little surprise. We are sitting naively on an economic powder keg. Explosive population in the countries that can least afford it will put one of the final nails in the coffin of nations already teetering on the edge of economic collapse. In many countries land, once fertile, has now become blowing desert sand, thus depriving once highly productive countries of exportable commodities, and making them recipients of the charity of donor nations.

Meanwhile, new global bureaucracies—from the World Trade Organization to the International Monetary Fund—are being established to handle the growth of the world's new financial markets. Martin Waller, bureau chief of the *Guardian* in England, says recent attempts by the G-7 nations to tame the global markets may have the effect of "anointing a market pontiff whose reach transcends old sovereignties." Translation: The New Economic Order is coming. The apparatus is nearly in place for central planning on a global scale. But, as with most radical plans, it will surely be preceded by a crisis of enormous proportions—in all probability, a worldwide recession. Watch for it. Read the business section of your morning paper with the discernment that comes with "new eyes," because the signs of global economic chaos are on the horizon. But again, the truth of the future was not left unexplored by the wisdom of the past.

One example of how the Bible has always been ahead of its time can be found in James 5:1–8:

> "Go to now, *ye* rich men, weep and howl for your miseries that shall come upon *you.* Your riches are corrupted, and your garments are moth eaten. Your gold and silver is cankered; and the rust of them shall be a witness against you, and shall eat your flesh as it were fire. Ye have heaped treasure together for the last days. Behold, the hire of the labourers who have reaped down your fields, which is of you kept back by fraud, crieth: and the cries of them which have reaped are entered into the ears of the Lord of Sabaoth. Ye have lived in pleasure on the earth, and been wanton; ye have nourished your hearts, as in a day of slaughter. Ye have condemned *and* killed the just; *and* he doth not resist you. Be patient therefore, brethren, unto the coming of the Lord. Behold, the husbandman waiteth for the precious

fruit of the earth, and hath long patience for it, until he receive the early and latter rain. Be ye also patient; stablish your hearts: for the coming of the Lord draweth nigh."

The machinations of a world government, and its enormous global economic repercussions, are upon us. Nations which once thought they controlled their own destinies are now learning that they are little more than tiny cogs within a massive, out-of-their-control worldwide machine.

> **Will the locus of such a one-world government be the United Nations . . . on U.S. soil?**

It's anticipated by many that the locus of this future control will be the United Nations, a melting pot for one-world government and an internationalized, homogenized religion. Ostensibly, this new global arrangement is to be politically uncluttered, socially impartial, environmentally aware, and economically superior to the failed systems of the past. For many, it will look good on paper when, in fact, we're actually on a roller coaster that's just now making its slow ascent up a rickety, moribund structure, climbing inexorably to the top, only to accelerate on the way down on a ride designed to take our collective breaths away.

Still, the story is only half-told. During the anticipation of an approaching world government, there will also be a commensurate demonstration of pain, pestilence, and plagues—areas of concern we touched on in earlier chapters. So fasten your seat belts and mount your courage. The roller coaster is still struggling to the top, setting up all of humanity for a breakneck descent. . . . into the unknown.

# FAMINES, PLAGUES, AND PESTILENCE

"I ventured through that parish this day, to ascertain the condition of the inhabitants, and although a man not easily moved,
I confess myself unmanned by the extent and intensity of the
suffering I witnessed. More especially among the women and
little children, crowds of whom were to be seen scattered over
the turnip fields, like a flock of famished crows, devouring the
raw turnips, and mostly half naked, shivering in the snow and
sleet, uttering exclamations of despair, whilst their children
were screaming with hunger."

—CAPTAIN WYNNE, INSPECTING OFFICER
WEST CLARE, 1846

WHAT CAPTAIN WYNNE WITNESSED that fateful day was the
terrible famine in Ireland that began with the first documented
potato blight on September 9, 1845. The nation had become
dependent on the potato for the major portion of its diet, but
when a fungus—for which there is still no remedy—destroyed
the potato crop that year, Ireland starved. The most conservative

tally reported one-and-a-half million dead, with an additional one million survivors. Many of those left their beloved, beleaguered island, destined for a better life in America.

## FAMINE DEFINED

BY DEFINITION, a *famine* is a shortage of food of sufficient duration to cause widespread privation and a rise in mortality. And while the recurrence of famine in our day is front-page news, famines have been the bane of humanity since at least as early as the beginnings of agriculture itself. Little is known of the frequency and severity of famines in the past, but history is filled with stories of this phenomenon—no fewer than ten famines are mentioned in the Bible—while an actual accounting of these natural disasters remains incomplete, and quantification sketchy. Even within our own century, the exact number of people who have perished during times of famine is unknown.

> No fewer than ten famines are mentioned in the Bible.

Historically, periodic drought has been most crippling in the more arid areas of densely populated Asia, especially in China and India, and has contributed to the cycle of famine and death of whole populations in those countries. Chronic pest infestations and epidemics of plant and animal diseases have also been significant natural causes of famine. The well-known potato blight that struck Ireland in the 1840s, is perhaps the best known.

Introduced into Ireland in the eighteenth century from South America, the potato proved an ideal crop, and by the end of the 1700s was responsible for some 80 percent of the calories in the Irish peasant diet. The mysterious fungus, however, appeared three times in the 1840s, each time destroying most of the potato crop. Relief efforts mounted were only partially effective, with more than one-and-a-half million casualties. Interestingly, with 4.9 million people, today's Irish population still remains much lower than its 1840 level.

## WAR AND POLITICALLY-INDUCED FAMINES

WARFARE FROM EARLIEST times has also been a primary contributor to the destruction of crops and animals, and subsequent blockades and attacks on cities and ports have been responsible for countless famines. These were some of the reasons for the hundreds of thousands of deaths in Leningrad, Warsaw, the Netherlands, and Greece during World War II. Two of the most savage recent instances of war-induced famine resulted in up to five million dead in China's Honan province in 1943, and untold suffering in Cambodia (Kampuchea) in the late 1970s. Today Rwanda, Burundi, and other African nations hang on the edge of survival due to this same savage military phenomenon.

Often, famine is induced by the jackboots and hate of police and military suppression. Throughout history, control of a nation's food supply has been used with bloody, surgical precision by political leaders to force their will during peacetime. (Remember Somalia?) One horrendous twentieth-century example is the Soviet famine of the early 1930s, which was the result of a merciless drive to force bands of reluctant peasants onto collective farms. The Soviet oppressors achieved their objective, but at a human cost beyond description.

## THE POOR SUFFER MOST

WHEN FAMINE STRIKES, all citizens within a given area do not necessarily suffer equally. The rich often escape the consequences of famine because they either control the source of food, have the wherewithal to hoard it, or possess the mobility to move to other less-threatened areas. However, when food scarcity causes a rise in prices, the poor and their families find access to food cut off. One example was the terrible Bengal famine of 1943, which had many causes: the conquest of Burma by the Japanese, which deprived India of its traditional source of surpluses; the removal of rice stocks from rural

Bengal to deny them to potential enemies; a series of hurricanes that reeked havoc on the main 1942 harvest; and an unprecedented war-induced prosperity in Calcutta.

These factors combined to bring about a six-fold increase in the price of rice. The wealthy—and those who could find jobs in town—were little affected. For most people, however, food prices were utterly beyond reach. Estimates of the number who perished in that terrible famine range between one-and-a-half and three million. It's a pattern that has continued to this day.

## THE NEWS DOESN'T GET MUCH BETTER

WITH THAT AS a brief background, let's look at what famine is doing to desperately needy people right now. I wish I could report that with an exploding agricultural technology worldwide, things called "famines" no longer exist. But such a report would be a lie.

I wish I could tell you the distribution of food worldwide has finally become equitable, with the rich sharing abundantly with the poor, the haves giving of their abundant means to the desperate have-nots, with the result being one big, happy, well-fed family of nations. But it wouldn't be true.

I wish I could bring you the good news that a little African boy named Yacouba no longer has to face the horrors of famine, that no more must he struggle for survival by eating boiled tree bark and roots, and that he is no longer forced to pillage anthills to steal grain kernels insects have stored away. But it isn't so.

I wish I could tell you that impoverished Peruvian peasants, unschooled beggar children on the streets of Bogota, and favela-dwellers in Rio have now turned an economic corner, and that hunger, pain, and despair are no longer on their menu. But the reality is far different.

For the majority of our world's population, the bad news is that things are worse today than ever. And, as we approach the new millennium, it's going to become even less pleasant for hundreds of millions more.

## GOD'S WORD PROPHESIES FAMINES

ONCE AGAIN, God's Word states unequivocally what we can expect as we approach the end times. One of the most significant prophetic passages of Scripture is found in Matthew 24: 1–8. It has more relevance than an updated "famine report" viewed on the television news, or the editorials we read in our daily papers. Hear the Word of the Lord:

> "And Jesus went out, and departed from the temple: and his disciples came to *him* for to show him the buildings of the temple. And Jesus said unto them, See ye not all these things? verily I say unto you, There shall not be left here one stone upon another, that shall not be thrown down. And as he sat upon the mount of Olives, the disciples came unto him privately, saying, Tell us, when shall these things be? and what *shall be* the sign of thy coming, and of the end of the world? (The literal Greek translation is "the end of the Age of Grace before the Millennial Age under Messiah begins.") And Jesus answered and said unto them, Take heed that no man deceive you. For many shall come in my name, saying, I am Christ; and shall deceive many. And ye shall hear of wars and rumours of wars: see that ye be not troubled: for all *these things* must come to pass, but the end is not yet. For nation shall rise against nation, and kingdom against kingdom: and there shall be famines, and pestilences, and earthquakes, in divers places. All these *are* the beginning of sorrows."

## A HURTING, HUNGRY WORLD

EVERY YEAR, thirteen to eighteen million people die from hunger and starvation. Every twenty-four hours, 35,000 human beings die from hunger and hunger-related diseases. The number of people who die every two days of hunger and starvation is equivalent to the number who were killed instantly by the bombing of Hiroshima. And there's no sign of better days to come.

> Every twenty-four hours, 35,000 human beings die from hunger. . . .

Strong demand for food in China is exacerbating a dwindling supply of grain worldwide. The 1.2 billion Chinese need to eat, and even with its strict control of the number of children per family, the population of the largest nation on earth continues to explode.

Droughts in Australia and North Africa, along with heavy rains in the United States, are also contributing to the problem. But the huge demand in China represents an unprecedented crisis, according to Lester Brown of the Worldwatch Institute. Brown describes China as "a huge sponge," buying up for its developing population every food commodity the rest of the world can produce. While China makes its increasing demands for food, poor nations that do not have the foreign exchange will continue to go hungry.

Kazakhstan, the main exporter of grain in the former Soviet Union, is suffering a diminished harvest—the lowest in decades. As a result, Kazakhstan will not be exporting any grain, tightening a worldwide supply, and exacerbating a particularly desperate situation in Russia and central Asia. And this is only the tip of the iceberg.

## IT'S ALREADY TOO LATE FOR MILLIONS

OVER A BILLION of our world's inhabitants are going to bed hungry every night. That's because famine is an individual problem. Those who are desperately hungry, with no food in sight, are victims of famine, and join a global fraternity of the doomed. Thousands are dying painful deaths, while hundreds of thousands more are too numb with hunger even to realize their pain

A single stark paragraph in *U.S. News & World Report* has described hunger and starvation in these graphic terms: "First the belly swells, then the hair turns gray and the skin cracks; after a while the victim dies in mute misery."

Sadly, such an experience will soon be the fate of millions.

A biochemist at Stanford University in Palo Alto, California, has reported, "It is already too late to prevent famines that will kill millions. Already, one-half billion are starving and another billion are malnourished. There is no possible solution in the near future, because it is too late to produce enough food." These statistics are frightening enough. What's worse is that the numbers may actually now be conservative.

> Over a billion of our world's inhabitants are going to bed hungry. . . .

## WHO ARE THE HUNGRY?

THE STATISTICS RELATED to the pain of world hunger and poverty boggle the mind. As you review these numbers, I remind you that behind every "fact" about hunger is a man, woman, or child who will not have enough food in his or her stomach tonight.

- Hunger, according to some experts, plagues nearly one billion people around the globe.

- No famine, flood, earthquake, or pestilence has ever claimed the lives of a quarter of a million children a week. Malnutrition does that every seven days.

- Two out of every eleven people in the world are hungry most of the time, especially during times of seasonal food scarcity.

- Sixty million are on the verge of extinction in Africa because of starvation.

- About three hundred million are chronically hungry throughout Asia.

- More than seventy million people live in poverty, and fifty million in absolute poverty in the countries of Latin America.

- One-third of all the grain in the world, and one-half of the fish caught, are fed to animals in the wealthier nations.

- Worldwide, upwards of 1.2 billion people live in absolute poverty, which is due largely to hunger, famine, sickness, and disease.

Again, I wish I could come up with a positive minority report stating that all will be well in the days ahead. I wish that with a snap of my fingers I could reverse the pain of hunger and disease for the world's children. Instead, I'm compelled to turn to the pages of God's Word for counsel and truth about the future. Three such verses are found in Revelation, Matthew, and Ezekiel:

> "And I looked, and behold a pale horse: and his name that sat on him was Death, and Hell followed with him. And power was given unto them over the fourth part of the earth, to kill with sword, and with hunger, and with death, and with the beasts of the earth."
>
> —REVELATION 6:8

> "For nation shall rise against nation, and kingdom against kingdom: and there shall be famines, and pestilences, and earthquakes, in divers places."
>
> —MATTHEW 24:7

> "A third part of thee shall die with the pestilence, and with famine shall they be consumed in the midst of thee: and a third

part shall fall by the sword round about thee; and I will scatter a third part into all the winds, and I will draw out a sword after them."

—EZEKIEL 5:12

## A WORLD IN PERIL OF NEW DISEASES

THE WORD OF God remains sure and true. It is—and has always been—an accurate prediction of events to come. Not to believe its pages is to court personal, regional, and national disaster. Yet few believe the words of God, whether they be about famine, hunger, poverty, or the plagues that have already descended upon humanity. Once relatively rare, these pestilences have destroyed our best and brightest, reducing us to less than the creatures God designed us to be. And even as we continue to toy with a fragile, ultimately unforgiving ecosystem for our own profit and greed, we reap the whirlwind of pain and personal poverty.

The World Health Organization laments that the planet is threatened by a host of new and resurgent diseases. "The world is not becoming a safer place," says Dr. David Heymann, director of the Division of Emerging Diseases. "It's clear that an outbreak of disease anywhere must now be perceived as a threat to all countries, and despite many warnings, we are not fully equipped to contain them."

*. . . the planet is threatened by a host of new and resurgent diseases.*

Heymann, who leads the organization's effort to control the Ebola virus in Zaire, is now particularly concerned with bubonic plague, hantavirus, Lyme disease, tuberculosis, and drug-resistant strains of gonorrhea. But as virulent as these diseases are, virtually no malady takes center stage as does AIDS.

## AIDS UPDATE

THE LATEST ESTIMATE by the United Nations is that approximately two million Africans will die of AIDS within the next five years. The fifteen countries hardest hit by the deadly virus will be Botswana, Burundi, Cameroon, Congo, Ethiopia, Ivory Coast, Ghana, Kenya, Malawi, Rwanda, Tanzania, Uganda, Zaire, Zambia, and Zimbabwe. But as tragic as this is for these many African nations, the crisis goes far beyond that continent. It's also claiming lives in Asia, Europe, Latin America, and in the islands of the sea. Even the head of the Indian Health Association is now predicting ten thousand deaths per day in India alone because of AIDS by the year 2000.

But it's not necessary to travel to Africa or India to be assaulted by such overwhelming statistics. How about what's happening in the United States? Dr. Stanley Montieth, an expert on AIDS, says the disease is the greatest tragedy ever to befall America in strictly human terms. Comparing the numbers of people with HIV, the nation will lose far more people from those already infected than were lost in the Revolutionary War, the Civil War, the Spanish-American War, World War I, World War II, Korea, Vietnam, and the Gulf War combined.

Montieth reminds us that, when all those infected today die, it will not mark the end of this epidemic. In fact, he warns, it will be just the beginning. And no cure or effective treatment is in sight. Scientists now believe the AIDS virus becomes resistant to many members of a class of drugs if it is exposed to just one of them. In other words, treating patients with one protease inhibitor may make others useless against the disease.

## INFECTIOUS DISEASES ON THE RAMPAGE

A GENERATION AGO, thanks to immunizations and better, stronger drugs, scientists confidently predicted the demise of infectious diseases. However, such illnesses have not only refused to go away, they have actually increased in the United States by 58 percent since 1980, according to the latest data.

While much of that increase can be attributed to the AIDS virus, more people are also dying of common infections such as pneumonia. The increase also reflects the emergence of lethal new infections, the reemergence of nasty old ones, and a growing resistance to antibiotics.

The World Health Organization says bacteria resistant to common antibiotics represent the most serious threat to the global medical community for the foreseeable future. "The problem is getting out of hand, and the implications are devastating," said a spokesman for WHO. "It is costing billions each year to keep drug-resistant strains under control, and one is seeing resistance in all manner of diseases. For some, there is no effective treatment."

A generation ago . . . scientists confidently predicted the demise of infectious diseases.

To make matters worse, global incidences of cholera, tuberculosis, diphtheria, and bubonic plague have all increased dramatically during the past five years. The mosquito-borne illness, dengue, which produces deadly fevers, has now appeared in Latin America and the Caribbean for the first time in more than two decades.

When men inspired by God penned the holy Scriptures, AIDS, cancer, dengue fever, and the many diseases common today were unknown. But over time, man's sin brought havoc upon himself, and much of that havoc took the form of increasing physical afflictions. Men and women set themselves up as the measure of all things. They chose to be the center of their own universe. They gave up God-ordained virtues for the desires of the flesh. They took from, added to, and chose to deny God's Truth, thus further compromising their position with their Creator. Surely such historic activity lies behind the words we read in Revelation 22:18: "For I testify unto every man that heareth the words of the prophecy of this book, If any man shall add unto these things, God shall add unto him the plagues that are written in this book."

## Mystery Virus

Perfectly healthy people in Argentina are being struck down by a mysterious virus. The best guess now is that the disease may be a strain of hantavirus pulmonary syndrome which has also been showing up recently in the American southwest, brought on by an explosion within the rat population.

These rodents are carrying strains closely related to the bubonic plague which nearly wiped out the population of Europe in the fourteenth century, killing one-fourth to one-half the popu-lation, or about seventy-five million people. History is already repeating itself, with the worse yet to come.

## Diphtheria Outbreak

Our litany of physical horrors continues as we now learn that an epidemic of diphtheria is sweeping the former Soviet Union. It's so serious, say public health officials, that it could have a very real destabilizing effect on countries already hit with economic and social dislocation.

The outbreak began in Moscow and St. Petersburg, and has now spread to virtually every region of Russia.

At last report, the diphtheria is now hitting the Ukraine, Belarus, Moldova, Azerbaijan, Armenia, Georgia, Kazakhstan, Tajikistan, Turkmenistan, and Uzbekistan. The disease kills 10 percent of its victims, and is already infecting hundreds of thousands. All this reminds us that we have entered the age of plagues and pestilence once and for all, just as the Bible prophesied.

While we must be deeply concerned, and do all we can to ameliorate these conditions that affect—and infect—so many, at the same time, we must be vigilant. We should be well aware that the final minutes on the clock are ticking away, that plagues worse than these will continue to descend on all our houses, and that the final stage is being further prepared for the return of Jesus Christ and the subsequent events of the millennium.

It has all been recorded for those who have eyes to see. Zechariah 14:12 reminds us, "And this shall be the plague wherewith the LORD will smite all the people that have fought against Jerusalem; Their flesh shall consume away while they stand upon their feet, and their eyes shall consume away in their holes, and their tongue shall consume away in their mouth."

Revelation 9:1–6 is of particular significance here:

"And the fifth angel sounded, and I saw a star fall from heaven unto the earth: and to him was given the key of the bottomless pit. And he opened the bottomless pit; and there arose a smoke out of the pit, as the smoke of a great furnace; and the sun and the air were darkened by reason of the smoke of the pit. And there came out of the smoke locusts upon the earth: and unto them was given power, as the scorpions of the earth have power. And it was commanded them that they should not hurt the grass of the earth, neither any green thing, neither any tree; but only those men which have not the seal of God in their foreheads. And to them it was given that they should not kill them, but that they should be tormented five months: and their torment *was* as the torment of a scorpion, when he striketh a man. And in those days shall men seek death, and shall not find it; and shall desire to die, and death shall flee from them."

## NEW TB EPIDEMIC IN EUROPE

"AND THERE SHALL BE famines . . . in divers places . . ." Matthew 24:7. A new epidemic of a drug-resistant strain of tuberculosis has broken out in eastern and central Europe, according to World Health Organization sources. The countries hit hardest to date include Hungary, Armenia, Moldava, Lithuania, and Romania. At least 29,000 people have died of TB in this region

> . . . TB kills some three million people a year worldwide. . . .

in the last year with more than two million infected. (And we thought TB was a thing of the past.) WHO sources now say that TB kills some three million people a year worldwide, but that this latest outbreak in Europe could claim more than thirty million lives unless immediate action is taken.

Meanwhile, there are still other ominous signs:

- AIDS continues to affect an estimated six thousand new victims a day throughout the world.

- A man with radical white supremacist views was arrested in Columbus, Ohio, for allegedly obtaining bubonic plague bacteria through the mail.

- Three distinct strains of Ebola, the deadly virus that liquefies human organs and tissue, have now been identified. They include Ebola Zaire, Ebola Sudan, and Ebola Reston. To date, scientists still do not know the disease's natural host, though monkeys and chimpanzees are known carriers.

- More people are contracting sexually transmitted diseases (STDs) than previously thought—a trend that is increasing the threat of AIDS on a worldwide scale. At least 333 million people will be stricken with STDs, such as syphilis and gonorrhea, an increase from the 250 million new cases estimated.

- A new federal survey of people with pneumococcal infections found that 25 percent had strains resistant to penicillin—the once nearly infallible treatment in killing the bugs.

## No Safe Havens?

WHAT DO THESE disasters portend for the future of our world? Will wars, crime, disease, plagues, and sexual perversion continue their furious march across the United States, and around the globe like a blazing, unstoppable prairie fire of evil and despair? Will there be no safe haven on earth? Where are the events we've been discussing taking us?

Well, it's all something that should surprise no one—especially those familiar with Bible prophecy, which explains just how badly conditions on earth will deteriorate in the days just before Jesus returns. Are such plagues happening because of mankind's pursuit of iniquity? You be the judge.

"This also know," wrote Paul in 2 Timothy 3:1–5, ". . . that in the last days perilous times shall come. For men shall be lovers of their own selves, covetous, boasters, proud, blasphemers, disobedient to parents, unthankful, unholy, Without natural affection, trucebreakers, false accusers, incontinent, fierce, despisers of those that are good, Traitors, heady, highminded, lovers of pleasures more than lovers of God; Having a form of godliness, but denying the power thereof: from such turn away."

The actions of humanity reveal that we've somehow missed the boat and gotten our priorities out of whack. By our consistent, stubborn actions to pretend we are boss, we exhibit the various Old Testament meanings for the word sin, which means: "to miss the mark; to have a spirit of perversity or iniquity; to transgress or trespass; to be evil." Our modern world is hurtling irresistibly toward a deadly destination, and there seems to be no way to turn back.

Several years ago, author Thomas Wolfe reminded his readers, "You can't go home again." Sure, you and I have tried to turn back the clock in a thousand ways, but it has never worked. We've attempted to reinvent the wheel of past relationships. We have gone back to recapture the good old days. We have struggled to make a good omelet from bad eggs. We have tried to fool ourselves into believing the impossible, while hanging onto the inane. But it has never worked.

Thomas Wolfe's colorful character, George Webber, said,

". . . You can't go back home to your family, back home to your childhood, back home to romantic love, back home to a young man's dreams of glory and fame, back home to exile . . . back home to lyricism . . . back home to the ivory tower, back home to places in the country . . . back home to the father you have lost and have been looking for, back home to someone who can help you, save you, ease the burden for you, back home to the old forms and systems of things which once seemed everlasting but which are changing all the time—back home to the escapes of Time and Memory."

## BAD NEWS AND GOOD NEWS

NO, WE CAN'T GO BACK. And we can't return to our old homes. But we can prepare for a new, heavenly dwelling, one that will abide forever, as we sit in the presence of the King of kings, and Lord of lords. Jesus' own words in Matthew 24, Mark 13, and Luke 17 and 21 leave little doubt that we are poised at the very threshold of cataclysmic change. We're told to continue to watch for certain signs of the times—the advent of false prophets, widespread religious deception, international upheaval, an increase in great earthquakes, an even great onslaught of devastating plagues, famines, and strange phenomena in the heavens, along with changing global weather patterns.

One hardly needs to be a Bible scholar or student of prophecy to see these signs in the world today. We need only pick up our newspapers and read of the rampant religious deception that abounds. A mindless humanism preaches the corrupt notion that man—not God—is at the center of the universe. Man—not God—should be at the center of our schools, and civic life. Man—not God—is the "force" from whom all earthly blessings flow. This dogma of deceit is not only with us, but it is gaining power and influence at home and abroad, reminding us daily that we have truly entered the post-Christian era.

> The Good News is Jesus is coming back very soon.

The bad news is that circumstances are going to become more vile and repulsive in the days ahead—even worse than what we've reviewed in these pages so far.

The Good News is Jesus is coming back very soon.

But before He returns, there will be increasing numbers of signs to announce His coming, giving us graphic reminders that we will indeed see Him face-to-face as we meet Him at edge of eternity.

## 7

## WORLD EVENTS THAT SIGNAL
## THE END TIMES: PART I

**T**HE SIGNS OF JESUS' COMING are everywhere: The falling away from scriptural truth, the rise of neo-paganism and occultism, the persecution of believers, the unbridled support of the "religion" of humanism where man is the measure of all things, and the pantheistic adoration of nature. All these trends are leading inevitably to the formation of a new global belief system.

Ultimately, the Bible reveals, this will result in one man exalting himself "above all that is called God, or that is worshipped; so that he sitteth in the temple of God." This year, we moved a step closer to that prophetic fulfillment. And as we advance toward the new millennium, there will be even greater attempts in the evolution of a new false global spirituality, whether we are consciously aware of it or not.

Sometimes you and I fight against the oppression of time lines and daily schedules. We can easily read the parable in the first book of the New Testament of the workers in the vineyard, and quickly evaluate its meaning as there's no reason to hurry; we have all the time in the world. But this story must be placed in contrast to another story found in the same gospel about a wedding party that failed to prepare in time for the party. This is the story to look at seriously.

We must remember that Jesus viewed history as a continuum —a straight historical line with a beginning, and an end—a distinctly Jewish point of view. Most of us living in the last hours of the twentieth century do not enjoy seeing life or history from that view. We would rather not be reminded—even though we know in our hearts it is true—that some day in the future there will be a final reckoning, a balancing of the accounts, a time when there will be no tomorrow. That day of finality is soon upon us, because the signs of Jesus' coming are everywhere.

So, you may ask, what are some additional, vital signs for which Jesus instructed us to be vigilant? I would suggest a tremendous, ever-new explosion of knowledge. The wonders of the exploration of outer space. War in space. The exponential flow of information, the foundation being established for one world government, and $$$ vs. 666. Let's look at a few of these events that fulfill ancient prophecy and will usher in the millennium.

## THE KNOWLEDGE EXPLOSION

DANIEL 12:4 declares, "But thou, O Daniel, shut up the words, and seal the book, *even* to the time of the end: many shall run to and fro, and knowledge shall be increased." This prophecy has been, and is being, fulfilled before our eyes with meticulous accuracy.

The Book of Daniel was to be sealed, and its contents kept incomprehensible, until the time of the end. Isn't it strange that expositions of this book were not attempted until recent times? No expositor made any published attempt to explain Daniel, verse by verse, until the twentieth century. (Luther tried but was unsuccessful.) Then, again, this time of the end would also witness tremendous strides in international travel and knowledge. This is happening. What's interesting is that the two predictions are interrelated. Because of our undeniably prolific explosion of knowledge, tourists are able to hop from continent to continent, while astronauts whiz through the universe.

## FROM HORSES TO HIGH-SPEED COMPUTERS

EARLY MAN traveled at the rate of thirty miles per hour, for a limited period of time, on horseback. Centuries passed and the human race continued to cry, "Giddy-up!" Then, in 1913, Henry Ford built his first Model-T. This vehicle attained the fantastic speed of twenty-five miles per hour—slower than a horse, but able to run for hours. Soon the genius of man increased automobile speeds to 120 miles per hour. Today, race-car enthusiasts have smashed records, hitting the astronomical rate of more than 600 miles per hour at the Bonneville Salt Flats. "Bullet" trains in Japan fulfill the to-and-fro prediction of Daniel for the end times, as does the French Concorde jet, which crosses the Atlantic at more than 2,000 miles per hour. Spaceships rocket along at 24,000 miles per hour. Speed is what we are all about, and it is inescapably tied to mankind's frantic search for and extraordinary increase in knowledge.

> Speed is what we are all about. . . .

Library shelves display that knowledge. The *Encyclopedia Britannica* has to print a volume of newly accumulated information every year. And now, with the world's access to the Internet and the proliferation of "Home Pages," information is updated by on-line sources daily—even hourly, in some cases.

Medical people own special transmitters which keep them up-to-date on the latest international reports concerning recent discoveries. Scientists remind us that knowledge is doubling every two-and-one-half years—perhaps faster.

Computers are so highly developed that when the Apollo 13 mission was nearly aborted because the ship became crippled in space, a mere eighty-four minutes were required to discover the problem. A person with pencil and paper would have needed a million years to solve the same problem. It's exponentially even faster today.

As fantastic as all this may seem, we must also remember that a person can now cross the ocean within seconds by direct-dialing. In fact, we've been told that the number of overseas telephone calls has jumped from 900,000 to 191 million in thirty years. And I'm confident that statistic is already hopelessly out of date, because now with the Internet phone, even more millions are calling up friends, associates, and "on-line chat partners" virtually everywhere.

> "Yea, let God be true, but every man a liar."
> —Romans 3:4

In addition, by simply pushing a button on a television remote, a person can view a live sports event in California as he or she sits at home in Connecticut, or can watch a boxing match in Africa over a TV set in Arizona. And it's going to get faster. The hours of international television traffic via satellite have skyrocketed from zero in 1950 to eighty in 1965 to 7,887 in 1975 to 28,393 in 1980 and is still soaring higher in the late 1990s.

This latter piece of information is especially interesting in light of one of the greatest prophecies contained in the Book of Revelation. During the tribulation hour, God's two witnesses will be killed and the entire world will view their bodies: "And they of the people and kindreds and tongues and nations shall see their dead bodies [the two witnesses] three days and an half, and shall not suffer their dead bodies to be put in graves" (Revelation 11:9). For centuries, Bible scoffers ridiculed such an idea. Today, television has silenced the uninformed and unenlightened who mock God's Word. In fact, we now can all easily comprehend how every eye shall see him [the Lord] when He returns to earth (see Revelation 1:7).

Since Christ's return will be to the Mount of Olives near Jerusalem, and since Middle East developments are being shown nightly via TV news, who can question the accuracy and reliability of God's Holy Word? Prophecy is being fulfilled, and skeptics will forever be forced to admit their shortsightedness. "Yea, let God be true, but every man a liar" (Romans 3:4). Through his scientific accomplishments, man has made it possible for Christ's return to be witnessed intentionally. The equipment is ready to telecast the greatest event of the ages. Stay tuned!

## WONDERS IN SPACE (YES, EVEN UFOS)

MEANWHILE, OTHER unbelievable activities are either happening or being planned for the heavens. For instance, two Voyager spacecraft were launched into the great beyond several years ago. Before they complete their journey, they will have traveled billions of miles. Their courses will have taken them past Jupiter and Saturn, and on past Uranus. Never in the history of the world have scientists had an opportunity for such close examination of the moons of these two planets. This is a "first," because no spacecraft from earth had ever made the billion-mile flight to Saturn. After passing Uranus, they will continue into outer space. If all goes well, the Voyagers will pass a star in 40,000 years—and 107,000 years later, a second star. All this is incredible in light of the fact that Jesus prophesied that the space age would signal His return to earth. This event of the ages must surely be at hand.

The predictions uttered by Christ nineteen hundred years ago never became a realty until the present day beginning with the launching of Russia's Sputnik I in 1957. Since then, hundreds of scientific probes have been rocketed into space. Investigative reporter Michael Brown, author of *The Final Hour,* says his research into unidentified flying objects and close encounters reveals that few if any of these experiences represent actual contact with extraterrestrials. Instead, he says, they are manifestations of spiritual phenomena.

"We're told in the Bible that Satan will send lying wonders in the air. I think there was one study that said as many as eight million Americans are claiming at some time in their lives to have been abducted by UFOs. If you look at the descriptions, it's classic demonology. These are entities that have weird eyes. They're little, mean-looking, and leave bad effects. They leave odors a lot of time, they can go through a wall, and they haunt you for the rest of your life.

"It's not like a craft coming from some other planetary system, visiting you once, taking a sample, and then heading back for home.

"Rather it's an on-going spiritualistic, or better still demonic phenomenon. I think we are seeing the actual manifestation and materialization of forces of good and evil in direct combat. We're on that battle ground, we're in the middle of that crossfire right now."

Have you noticed the spate of new articles, books, and Internet Web Sites that are dedicated to these wonders in the air?

## LIVING IN SPACE

KEEP YOUR EYES on the heavens. Soon people will be living in space colonies. In fact, it's now predicted that humans may reside in space cities before the year two thousand, or immediately after the beginning of the third millennium. This information came several years ago from University of Michigan scientist James London. Again, we look to the past to demonstrate how quickly scientific predictions have come true, or are about to be realized. "Space colonies could become reality in the 1990s. I am not trying to be sensational or feed science fiction fantasies to the public. Instead, I am reporting what reputable and recognized scientists already consider feasible," observed Professor London.

Professor London said that the colonization of space with artificial worlds "which would be miles in size and have tens of thousands of people at first and then escalate into millions, could be the consequence of the first space shuttle flights." When asked if this really could happen, he replied, "It is the consensus of the best scientists alive. Apollo explorations proved that materials found on the moon could be used in the construction of space colonies. They would be hollow, doughnut-shaped or cylindrical, and glass-enclosed."

He added that these self-sustaining colonies could eventually solve the earth's energy crisis. Presently, Japan is planning space cities for vacations. Given the Japanese propensity for golf, we can also assume their scientists are attempting to figure out how to defy gravity for the thousands of golf balls surely to be hit from the tees of intergalactic country clubs. The way things are progressing, it seems that nothing would be impossible.

> "I, John, saw the holy city, new Jerusalem, coming down from God out of heaven. . . .
> —Revelation 21:2

Such statements about space colonies should silence the skeptics. Twenty years ago, the Bible account of a space city was derided as the writing of a deranged mind. Today, the scoffers of God's Word have become the simpletons. Intelligent, educated scientists predict space cities similar to the one John envisioned nineteen hundred years ago in Revelation 21:2: "I, John, saw the holy city, new Jerusalem, coming down from God out of heaven, prepared as a bride adorned for her husband."

Verses 10 through 23 provide a detailed description of this celestial wonder. If people are presently designing such cities that will accommodate thousands and eventually millions, is there a reader alive who thinks for a moment that almighty God cannot keep a promise of a celestial city He gave to John nineteen centuries ago?

## WAR IN SPACE

JESUS ALSO SAID, in Luke 21:25, 26, "There shall be signs in the sun, and in the moon, and in the stars; and upon the earth distress of nations, with perplexity; the sea and the waves roaring; Men's hearts failing them for fear, and for looking after those things which are coming on the earth: for the powers of heaven shall be shaken."

What is it that causes people to panic as they watch the heavens? Could it be a space war just before Christ's return to earth? In a *Detroit News* article several years ago, entitled "U.S., Soviets Gear Up for Outerspace Wars," Edwin G. Pipp stated, "Russia and the U.S. are moving toward fighting future wars in space. The two superpowers now have the potential to wage space battles between unmanned satellites hundreds of miles above the earth. The possibility of conflict in space is real enough to convince the air force to seek 10.8 million dollars to protect America's satellite systems from possible Soviet efforts to destroy or disable them. And the air force is spending even more millions for U.S. offensive space systems."

Then there was a détente between the United States and Russia, right? No more bellicose statements, right? No more animosity between the two nations, we've been told. But keep reading your daily paper, because what was predicted several years ago may still come to pass, especially as a weakened and threatened Russia again flexes its nuclear muscle.

One of those earlier predictions by *U.S. News & World Report* said: "Satellite killers, laser artillery, space cruisers—the stuff of today's science fiction—could revolutionize tomorrow's battlefield. American and Soviet scientists are racing to perfect ray guns and killer satellites that may turn outer space into the kind of battleground once thought possible only in science fiction movies."

Another *U.S. News & World Report* article described military spy satellites already in use: "Some satellites now aloft are so sophisticated that, from one hundred miles out in space, they can identify an object as small as a grenade in the hand of a Russian soldier."

No wonder Jesus said that men's hearts would fail them from fear for looking after those things which would come on the earth, and that the powers of heaven would be shaken! In the light of all these articles, is it not interesting that the Bible, nineteen hundred years ago, predicted a space war for the end time? Revelation 12:7 states, "And there was war in heaven. . . ."

## INFORMATION AND WORLD CONTROL

WHAT LIES AHEAD for civilization? What does the Bible predict? Guided by the Holy Spirit, Daniel states in chapters 8 and 11 that knowledge and what we now recognize as scientific advancement will be used by an international despot to control the nations of the world. After the Rapture of the Church of Jesus Christ, this leader called the Antichrist will take control of a newly-built Jewish temple in the Holy Land. He will proclaim himself as the awaited Messiah and claim that he is God. Second Thessalonians 2:4 describes his action by stating that the Antichrist ". . . opposeth and exalteth himself above all that is called God, or that is worshipped; so that he as God sitteth in the temple of God, showing himself that he is God."

The world will accept his proclamations out of fear. Even as world war is about to be unleashed upon the earth, this global charmer will convince humanity that he has the answers to the world's ills—that he alone can bring peace. Thus, on the basis of peace negotiations between Israel and many nations (Daniel 9:27), he will be accepted.

I believe that the Antichrist will enslave and control earth's billions through a sophisticated computer fashioned in his likeness. Thus, he will be able to have all the facts on every member of the human race at his fingertips. With unerring precision, he will know who receives his orders, obeys his commands, and honors his laws. Modem computers are already storing information on members of the human race.

*Europe*, the magazine of the Common Market, as long ago as 1979 reported in its September/October issue, "European researchers will soon be linked through a unique system for computerized data the Direct Information Access Network for Europe (called DIANE). DIANE is to interconnect numerous nations through the most advanced computer and telecommunications devices. The system will include data networks from Community countries with the future possibility of incorporating networks of non-Community countries."

**The actual Euronet computer is located in Luxembourg.**

In a related article, *Europe* reported, "We will have access to one hundred computer banks around the world (My note: it's much greater now). The name and data relating to every individual in the Western world is stored in computer banks everywhere. All this information can be fed into the Euronet computer that the European Community locates at Brussels, Belgium." Only the computer links are in Brussels. The actual Euronet computer is located in Luxembourg.

## "666" AND SOME MIND-BOGGLING MATH

WHAT IS THE SPEED of such computers? *Computer Digest* states, "In one-half second, today's computers can debit two thousand checks to three hundred different bank accounts, or can examine one thousand electrocardiograms, or score one hundred fifty thousand answers on three thousand exams, or figure the company payroll for one thousand employees."

I believe the international dictator will use such a computer, fashioned after his likeness (see Revelation 13:14), to enslave the inhabitants of earth. He will effectively do this through commerce—the buying and selling of products. Again, these statistics are already out of date. The numbers are even more mind-numbing now. Revelation 13:16, 17 states, "And he causeth all, both small and great, rich and poor, free and bond, to receive a mark in their right hand, or in their foreheads: and that no man might buy or sell, save he that had the mark, or the name of the beast, or the number of his name."

This forthcoming computer of the ages will give the Antichrist all the information necessary for him to govern the world. Its memory bank will know the number, record, and history of every living person. This number will definitely include "666" in one manner or another (see Revelation 13:18).

After exhaustive research in thousands of volumes, I have come to believe it will be a prefix, such as 666-7, 666-300, etc. Every individual credit card number must have some differentiation to distinguish one person from another. If all credit cards were identical, there would be mass confusion. Similarly, there will be some variance along with the "666" marking.

Some students of Bible prophecy suggest that this number will actually be composed of the international, national, and area computer codes presently in use (or being implemented), plus an individual number such as the person's Social Security number. The present international computer code is "6," and this is anticipated to expand to "666." The national computer identification code for the United States is "110." Within our nation are many area codes presently used for telephone communication. Thus, by using each of these codes in sequence, ending with the Social Security or other assigned number, every man, woman, and child within our borders could be individually identified. Such a number might be 666-110-212-419-27-2738.

In a report on a startling mathematical equation which was worked out on computers, Colonel Henry C. MacQueen, Sr., of Saratoga, California, took the three six-digit units, which, with their permutations of numbers, came out to N-60, and multiplied them by three. I don't expect you to understand the depth of the statement any more than I do, unless you are technically-oriented. I simply state these numbers to show you that each of earth's billions of inhabitants could possess his or her own personal number through the permutations of the figures described as "666."

In fact, the computers arrived at the conclusion that 46,834,995,519,212,567,931,529,902,559,000 (that's forty-six nonillion, eight hundred thirty-four octillion, nine hundred ninety-five septillion, five hundred nineteen sextillion, two hundred twelve quintillion, five hundred sixty-seven quadrillion, nine hundred thirty-one trillion, five hundred twenty-nine billion, nine hundred two million, five hundred fifty-nine thousand) human beings could each have his or her own number. Six hundred sixty-six, with its permutations, fits the bill, even if trillions more should be born!

As a final note on computer development, this quote from the *St. Louis Post Dispatch:*

> "Mathematicians at the Weizmann Institute of Science in Israel and the Massachusetts Institute of Technology are working on a new cryptographic system and microcomputer chip that may be able to provide everyone in the world with a personal, unbreakable code. The goal is to ensure for privileged government, business, and personal communications the confidentiality threatened as never before by espionage of all sorts. . . . The new cryptographic technique. . . . is 'one of the surest means of concealment ever devised.'"

World computerization is so near that the international bankers, through "SWIFT" (Society for Worldwide Interbank Financial Telecommunications), have already done the legwork in preparing the way for the world leader to take control. Earlier, I mentioned one of the organizational leaders in Brussels, who stated, "We do not want another committee. We have too many already. What we want is a man of sufficient stature to hold the allegiance of the people, and to lift us out of the economic morass into which we are sinking. Send us such a man, and be he God or the devil, we will receive him."

This wish will soon be granted. A new "Hitler" with a monstrous computer to enslave millions, may soon take over the earth. All these events signal the imminent return of the Lord Jesus Christ.

### $$$ VERSUS "666"

THE WORLD'S CURRENT monetary system is creating havoc among bankers. In America alone, the annual check processing cost is well beyond $10 million. What a waste. Cash causes even greater problems as graft, bribery, corruption, and crime sweep the world. Leaders are crying, "Away with cash and eliminate crime!" American Bar magazine once reported that crime would be virtually eliminated if cash became obsolete. Cash is the only real motive for 90 percent of the robberies. Hence, its liquidation would create miracles in ridding earth's citizens of muggings and holdups.

This approach to the problem is spawning national experimentation. We are now being reminded that cashless buying has been approved in several states by the comptroller of the currency. If you read the articles on this subject in your newspaper, you'll learn that supermarkets, gas stations, variety and department stores all over the country are already testing the cashless bank account deduction plan for their customers. This is a portion of the Electronic Funds Transfer System which takes care of all one's needs through a number.

> Presently, no one knows how each of us spends our cash.

In connection with a cashless society, plans are being laid internationally to make a numbers system feasible. This explains the often bewildering lines and figures known as Universal Product Codes on virtually every item of merchandise sold today. The metric system is also being promoted and installed at a cost of billions of dollars by the international bankers. Their aim is the establishment of a one-world government. This government will control human beings through computerized numbers for all people. Presently, no one knows how each of us spends our cash. Once every transaction is credited to a person's number, however, "Big Brother" will know everything about everyone through computers.

## IT'S ALL IN THE NUMBERS

THE FOLLOWING REPORT was printed by *U.S. News & World Report* in April 1978. I'm referring to it again to ask you if you think anything may have changed during the twenty years since the article was first published.

> "Chances are your personal life is all on tape somewhere in the government's data banks. Now, Americans want more assurance that Washington will not use modern technology to harass or intimidate ordinary citizens. Available in government computers is a vast array of data on virtually every American, including personal finances, health, family status, and employment. For those who have ever had a brush with the law or been suspected of illegal activity, had a driver's license lifted, traveled abroad, or even hunted certain species of animals, the chances are that somebody, somewhere in the government has a record of this information. David F. Linowes, who headed the Privacy Protection Study Commission, asks: 'What happens if this data that is being collected gets into the wrong hands? There is no reason to believe that someone won't come along at some point in the future to abuse it.'"

What a profound statement in the light of Bible prophecy. And how much further along the road to "Big Brother is watching" than ever before. The new system is on the way, and its equipment is being built at break-neck speed. *Computer World's* Nancy French reported that the Society for Worldwide

Interbank Financial Telecommunication (called SWIFT) has completed its principal hardware and software selection for a communications network linking two hundred members worldwide. This system is so designed that any type of computer system in the world can become a participant. Again, these figures are changing so fast that they are without a doubt already obsolete.

## THE FUTURE IS HERE

ANY COMPUTER system in the world can be hooked into the mother computer in Luxembourg (whose major links are located in Brussels, Belgium). This information should be doubly interesting for the person with an interest in prophecy when one realizes that Brussels is the headquarters of the Common Market nations and NATO. In all probability, the present preparations may be part of the formation of the final ten-kingdom federation of nations prophesied in Daniel 2 and Revelation 13.

Let us now consider how the number "666" could become functional in such a mechanized society. Suppose every person in the world were assigned a single credit card and individual identification number? Bankers in the United States generally believe that most shoppers will exchange the wallet full of credit cards they now carry for a single, all-purpose card and number. Is this not already happening in some states?

We see, then, that a world number is feasible in the near future. However, there is a problem. A person could conceivably be kidnapped or killed for their numbered card. Because of this, some are advocating the insertion of a number on one's body—one that would not mar, scar, or detract from a person's features. It would be a laser beam tattoo, invisible to the human eye but clearly visible under infrared light.

You don't believe that such ideas are presently being suggested? Years ago I read a copy of *Senior Scholastic,* a newsmagazine used in American high schools, that pictured a group of young people with numbers on their foreheads. The photo was captioned, "The Future." Like it or not, understand it fully or not, the future is upon us. Revelation 13, describes the mark of the beast. Verse 18 tells us the rest: "Here is wisdom. Let him that hath understanding count the number of the beast: for it is the number of a man; and his number is Six hundred threescore *and* six."

Let's consider some of the most recent information available on this subject. It appeared on the front page of the *Chicago Tribune,* and it's shocking!

## NEW TECHNOLOGY EXPLOSION LEADING TO FUTURE 666 SYSTEM

"IN THE FUTURE tiny chip may get under skin" read the headline in the May 7, 1996 edition of the *Chicago Tribune*. Staff writer John Van reported, "A tiny chip implanted inside the human body to send and receive radio messages . . . is likely to be marketed as a consumer item early in the next century." He goes on to say that "several tecnologies already available or under development will enable electronics firms to make implantable ID locators, say futurists, and our yearning for convenience and security makes them almost irresistible to marketers." A sociology professor at Northwestern University said, "People accept that increased communications makes life more convenient at the same time that there's no hiding place anymore. If I have a universal ID implanted, I can cash a check anywhere in the world. There's no worry about credit cards being stolen. These are attractive matters."

> **Although the potential problems with locator ID chips are huge, they may be inevitable.**

A representative of the World Future Society said that although the potential problems with locator ID chips are huge, they may be inevitable. He said he believes that such chips will be voluntary at first but "things that are voluntary today have a way of becoming compulsory tomorrow."

Meanwhile, the *Wall Street Journal* reported a record trading day for the NASDAQ stock exchange on May 6, 1996 as a stock for a high-tech company, whose main asset is new biometric ID technology, soared overnight. The *Journal* said, "Comparator says the burst in trading volume is due to pent-up demand from plugged-in investors who knew that the release of the company's new line of 'biometric identity verification systems' was imminent."

The above secular sources confirm that the means now exist to usher in the infamous "Mark of the Beast" in which no human will be able to buy or sell without a "mark" or traceable implant (Revelation 13:16–18). Of course, this is not something for believers to fear as the actual "666" mark is activated after the wonderful event known as the Blessed Hope (Titus 2:13) or "Rapture [snatching away] of the Church, the believer's comfort (1 Thessalonians 4:16–18). Remember also that . . . "*God hath not given us the spirit of fear, but of power, and of love and of a sound mind*" (2 Timothy 1:7).

## THE FOUNDATIONS OF WORLD GOVERNMENT

ANOTHER EVENT that signals the end times is the beginning of a movement toward world government. You may wonder what may bring such a system into existence. I have no doubt that the spiraling inflationary trend will be the culprit. In fact, I believe a worldwide economic crisis looms on the horizon. This crisis may lead all of us into a world government under a Satan-dominated, one-world despot who manipulates humanity with his intentional computers. How close are we to such a government? The scene has been set in your lifetime and mine through the creation of the following international agencies:

1. *International Atomic Energy Agency (IAEA)*. The aim of this agency is to promote peaceful use of atomic energy. I fear the inevitable result will be to disseminate among foreign nations vital information on American atomic resources.

2. *International Labor Organization (ILO)*. The purpose of this arm of the one-world government is to coordinate labor demands throughout the world. It can also provide an ideal vehicle for the promotion of socialism and the one-world philosophy.

3. *Food and Agricultural Organization (FAO)*. This organization has been established to standardize food qualities and levels of nutrition internationally. It may well be the model instrument for implementing the Antichrist's law that no man might buy or sell without first receiving the mark of the beast (see Revelation 13:17).

4. *International Bank for Reconstruction and Development (World Bank)*. This international bureaucracy is designed to internationalize money standards. Ultimately it will place all the money power of the world in the hands of one giant agency. Already there is talk of issuing international currency under the direction of the United Nations.

5. *International Development Association (IDA)*. This one-world financing organization is responsible for establishing international control of natural resources.

6. *United Nations Educational, Scientific, and Cultural Organization (UNESCO)*. The purpose of this agency is to promote collaboration among nations through education, science, and culture. The ultimate aim, in the hands of the Antichrist, could be the complete integration of the races, plus leveling all world religions to a common plateau— thus making paganism, Christianity, socialism, off-beat religions, and a resurgent communism bosom bedfellows.

7. *World Health Organization (WHO)*. The internationalization of medicine, surgery, and the treatment of disease are the goals of this organization. It also can provide enormous political advantage to a world dictator because it provides a logical instrument for committing political opponents to hospitals for the mentally ill.

8. *International Finance Corporation (IFC)*. This organization is responsible for implementing a plan to take over the poorly developed areas of the world in order to bring smaller nations into subjection to a one-world government.

9. *International Monetary Fund (IMF)*. This fund will promote and expand international trade, standardize commerce and industry, and make it a simple matter for the Antichrist to issue his decree that no person can buy or sell without first receiving the mark of the beast.

10. *International Civil Aviation Organization (ICAO)*. This group has been established to standardize aviation laws, procedures, patterns, and practices throughout the world.

11. *Universal Postal Union (UPU)*. This agency promotes uniformity in postal services and the development of international collaboration—openly to promote the reciprocal exchange of mail. This may be the first step toward the international control of communications and censorship.

12. *International Telecommunications Union (ITU)*. The purpose of this organization is to provide international regulations for radio, telegraphic, and telephone services, thereby making the worldwide preaching of the gospel of Jesus Christ by means of radio and television a practical impossibility. (Christian broadcasting networks are already feeling the threat of disallowing them airwave rights in key areas of the world).

13. *World Meteorological Association (WMA).* The aim of this agency is to standardize and coordinate all meteorological work, weather information, and forecasts of the world. Weather control and climate modification are sinister possibilities.

14. *Inter-governmental Maritime Consultative Organization (IMCO).* This group promotes the coordination of international shipping, aiming to remove all discrimination by governments and all restrictive practices by shippers. Thus, international transportation will be under the control of another giant bureau which can dictate who and what can and cannot be served.

15. *International Trade Organization (ITO).* By tightening the terms of commerce and promoting the free flow of goods from one country to another under international agreement, ITO will have the capacity to break down national boundaries and pave the way for Satan's emperor, the Antichrist, to take control of the entire world.

16. *General Agreement on Tariffs and Trades (GATT).* The goal of this agency continues to be the subject of battles in the United States Congress. The fight centers on the lowering, or complete abolition, of all tariffs on foreign imports, the leveling of national boundaries, and the destruction of national royalties. Such actions would set the whole world up for allegiance to the beast.

The formation of these organizations has led outstanding thinkers to predict that a new world order is on the horizon. What do you think?

## INTERNATIONAL BANKING PLAN

SAUL H. MENDLOVITZ declares: "There is no longer a question of whether or not there will be a world government, for the declaration of interdependence is a part of the continuing drive to dilute, then dissolve, the sovereignty of the United States of America for the new world order, a new international economic order. Who is Saul H. Mendlovitz? He is director the the New World Order Models Project and Dag Hammerskjold Professor of Peace and World Order Studies at Rutgers Law School.

A leading member of the Council on Foreign Relations, James P. Warburg, told a U.S. Senate Foreign Relations Committee on February 7, 1950: "We shall have world government, whether we like it or not. . . . by consent or by conquest."

In 1960, there were virtually no courses being taught along the lines of world order in our universities. Today, there are between five hundred and one thousand colleges and universities teaching the new international order, all sponsored by the Rockefeller Foundation. All this planning does not come from the lips of impotent, powerless Utopians. Instead, the perpetrators of the world order are moving ahead by planning a new economic order.

Paul Scott had this group in mind when he reported the following in the Washington News Intelligence Syndicate: "The one-world perpetrators are calling for the development of a global policy on food and oil within the framework of the United Nations. It is their belief that by controlling food they can control people, and by controlling energy—especially oil—they can control nations and their financial systems. By placing food and oil under world control, along with the monetary system, they believe that they can have a world government operating. It is happening before our very eyes, in line with the predictions of the Bible."

## THE ENERGY CONTROVERSY

NOW IT IS EASY to see why the energy crunch ideology has been crammed down the throats of Americans and others in the world. Could this be an elaborate scheme to destroy paper money through an inflationary spiral that will make the nations submissive to a carefully planned economic system?

The *Washington Post* once reported, "The American public . . . never has taken the 'energy crisis' as seriously as do the politicians and technocrats of Washington, who periodically scold the nation for its ignorance or greed. The public skepticism is encouraged, if not fully confirmed, by the optimistic revisions in recent forecasts. Meanwhile, the world markets are glutted with oil."

> **The perpetrators of the new world order are moving ahead by planning a new economic order.**

I remember predicting these results more than fifteen years ago. Today, there is little doubt in the thinking person's mind that our past oil embargo and its resulting "crisis" thinking has affected the entire Western world and Eastern bloc of nations. Gasoline, coffee, doughnuts, and all staples are well more than double— even triple—the cost they were at the time of our oil crisis. However, each additional "crisis" adds to the vicious cycle of catastrophic events. In fact, we are on the same spiral Germany experienced from 1914 to 1922. It took only eight short years for their economic system to fail.

Read this chilling, firsthand report by C. M. Ripley who was on the scene at the time:

> "The collapse of German finance changed the nation into an economic madhouse. Gas bills were thirty times as high as rent costs. Prices were unbelievable. A pound of lard cost twenty million marks. A menu in a local restaurant offered the following: Two orders of roast goose, 160,000,000 marks; vegetables, 39,000,000 marks; tax, 69,000,000 marks, plus 20,000,000 marks for service. This would have been $131,432,000 American dollars before the war, including beverages. In stores, a box of matches cost three million marks, one raw egg, twelve million marks and a quart of milk ran thirty million marks on Tuesday and changed to forty million on Wednesday. The bill at Adlon

Hotel for six nights totaled two billion, 336 million marks. This would have been one-half million American dollars."

It was amazing how so much changed so fast. Everything was relatively normal in Germany in 1914. Butter sold for one-and-a-half marks per pound. However, by 1918 it had jumped to three marks—a 100 percent increase in four short years. Then the real problems began. By the spring of 1922, butter had risen to 2,400 marks per pound, by summer to 150,000 marks per pound, and by fall it had reached the astronomical figures of six million marks per pound, or the equivalent of one-and-a-half million American dollars.

I hasten to point out that we are on the same dangerous treadmill today. Suppose the results are the same as Germany experienced. This catastrophe would certainly usher in a new economic system for the world.

## WHEN CHRIST RETURNS

THE WORLD IS indeed preparing for more economic destabilization, increased political unrest, an outpouring of domestic and global violence such as we've never seen, all of which culminates in war and Armageddon. This conflict will be international as all nations come against Jerusalem, according to Zechariah 14:2. God's Word reveals the outcome. Zechariah 14:3, 4 reminds us, "Then shall the LORD go forth, and fight against those nations, as when he fought in the day of battle. And his feet shall stand in that day upon the mount of Olives, which *is* before Jerusalem on the east. . . ."

That passage describes the glorious return of the Lord Jesus Christ and His saints (the Christians who were raptured seven years earlier) to earth. The scene is also described in Revelation 19:11–21. When Christ returns, He, as the stone cut out without hands (Daniel 2:34 and 45), will smash all existing powers and set up His Kingdom. Then Daniel's interpretation of King Nebuchadnezzar's dream will be fulfilled in every detail.

But we have just begun to observe the signs of the end of the age. They are legion, and we will examine even more mind-stretching reports of natural phenomena, perpetrators of false peace, the increasing persecution of the Christian church around the world, and other immediate graphic signs of the end of the age that signal the Millennial Age and the return to earth of our Lord Jesus Christ.

It is simply incumbent on those with eyes to see, and ears to hear to recognize what is really going on as we inch ever closer to 2001, the edge of eternity.

# 8

## WORLD EVENTS THAT SIGNAL THE END TIMES: PART II

WRITING IN THE *Evangelical Beacon,* February 1993, Robert Moeller is on the mark. He accurately describes a general growing awareness among Christians that we are indeed living at the end of history's continuum. Moeller writes,

"The Persian Gulf Conflict was not the apocalyptic event many predicted, but it did start lots of people thinking about the fact that events do appear to be moving steadily in the direction of the end times. Putting aside calculations and calendars to examine recent world events, trends, and conditions, there are four global megatrends that coincide with Bible prophecy.

"First, there is the move toward a global economy, visible when changing conditions in Germany or Japan affect Wall Street within hours.

"The second megatrend is the rise of a united Europe. With tne disintegration of the Soviet Union and the demise of the Warsaw Pact, European unity is finally possible. NATO is waning, European economic boundaries have been dissolved, and a new military alliance is forming.

"Third is the isolation of Israel. Surrounding nations are becoming increasingly hostile, with even the United States acting judgmental and less friendly.

"Last is the collapse of Marxism in much of the world, with the People's Republic of China and North Korea being the last hold-outs. China has recently taken a step toward a market economy by establishing a Chinese stock exchange. The stage is being set for Christ's return and believers should use the new windows of opportunity for evangelism."

To understand these four "megatrends," accurately described by Moeller, they must be seen in the light of the prophecies found in Matthew 24. Jesus' prophecies are fully in sync with the headlines of the newspapers you and I read every day. And because this passage is the fulcrum on which we will build this chapter, let's look at it now. Matthew 24:3–14 reads,

"And as he sat upon the mount of Olives, the disciples came unto him privately, saying, Tell us, when shall these things be? and what *shall be* the sign of thy coming, and of the end of the world? And Jesus answered and said unto them, Take heed that no man deceive you. For many shall come in my name, saying, I am Christ; and shall deceive many. And ye shall hear of wars and rumours of wars: see that ye be not troubled: for all *these* things must come to pass, but the end is not yet. For nation shall rise against nation, and kingdom against kingdom: and there shall be famines, and pestilences, and earthquakes, in divers places. All these *are* the beginning of sorrows. Then shall they deliver you up to be afflicted, and shall kill you: and ye shall be hated of all nations for my name's sake. And then shall many be offended, and shall betray one another, and shall hate one another. And many false prophets shall rise, and shall deceive many. And because iniquity shall abound, the love of many shall wax cold. But he that shall endure unto the end, the same shall be saved. And this gospel of the kingdom shall be preached in all the world for a witness unto all nations; and then shall the end come."

With that as a key Scripture, we then move to 2 Peter 3, where we are given further instructions about how to live our lives in these perilous times. We are instructed not to react to the harrowing headlines with frustration, fear, and reckless living, as people who have no hope. Instead, under the current circumstances we are to live holy and godly lives; we are to make every effort to be spotless, blameless, and at peace; we are to be on our guard against error (some-

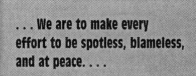

. . . We are to make every effort to be spotless, blameless, and at peace. . . .

thing we must be especially vigilant about, given the apostasy around which we will be surrounded until Christ comes); and we are to live and grow in the grace and knowledge of Jesus.

Even though future conditions on earth will worsen in every regard, Peter encourages us to anticipate the wickedness of the day, while at the same time reveling in the awareness that we will soon become active participants in a new heaven and a new earth.

In chapter 7 we recounted numerous world events that signal the end of the age. As you read that litany of "bad news," you may have thought, *Come on, Jack, enough is enough! There isn't too much more to shock and startle me, is there?* Well, I'm afraid there is a lot more. I don't offer all this information to depress you, but simply to help you become aware that as these events compound in their fury, you and I have been given the mandate to live blameless lives, at peace with God, growing daily in the grace and knowledge of Jesus Christ and His eternal truth—because soon we shall see Him face to face to give an account of our earthly pilgrimage (1 Corinthians 3:11–15; 1 John 2:28).

## GLOBAL AND DOMESTIC HOT SPOTS

BEFORE WE MOVE into greater detail on some of these occurrences, let's look at a list of political/governmental/economic/

societal "hot spots" that have enormous influence on end-time events. Even though this information will have changed somewhat by the time you read this page, the events described here will still be making their impact on our world as we move closer to the year 2001, and the edge of eternity.

- U.S.–Russian relations are at a post–cold war low, as Moscow resumes its historical imperial role, and, once again, longingly eyes the oil fields of the Middle East.

- Russian intelligence is building up its infrastructure on the island nation of Cyprus as a base of operations for its activities in the Middle East. Watch this build-up closely. It will have major repercussions for Israel.

- Iran is moving some of its terrorist training camps from Sudan to Angola. Africa has always been a seedbed for revolution. This is just the beginning of more international conflict.

- Global warming is melting the snows on the vast Tibet-Qinghai plateau, the source of the Yangtze River in western China. This will contribute to what may be the worst flooding disaster this century. Floods are predicted as a major end-time event.

- The U.S. and other developed countries are falling further behind in the war on drugs, according to intelligence agencies. The enemy of America may indeed lie within. Do you see a solution in sight?

- The U.S. Navy's use of an officer's Christian affiliation and beliefs to buttress its argument that he should be discharged from the service is growing evidence of official anti-Christian bias. Lieutenant. Commander Kenneth Carkhuff, a helicopter pilot, was discharged after he voiced opposition to women in combat. If this anti-Christian bias continues here at home, where in the rest of the world will the Christian act of faith be accepted and appreciated?

- Some of those suspected of participating in the bombing of the World Trade Center had even bigger plans—including blowing up eleven U.S. airliners on the same day. Global and domestic terrorism has been predicted in the Scriptures, and we're just seeing the tip of the iceberg.

- Scientists monitoring volcanic activity in the Mammoth Lakes area of California have measured an increase in carbon dioxide emissions—a sign of possible eruption. The Mammoth region is a highly volcanic area, and now some scientists speculate that an eruption there could have catastrophic effects as far away as Los Angeles. Earthquakes are a major precursor to the end of the world as we have come to know it. Look for more earthquakes, and with greater frequency. The largest quake in world history is prophesied in Revelation 16:18. But even then, the world will not end (Isaiah 45:17).

- More news from Big Brother: The Pentagon has unveiled a $10 million saucer-shaped reconnaissance plane that will be able to detect a basketball on the ground from 45,000 feet high, even in poor weather conditions. If the Pentagon can do this, how secure are you and your interests from an invasion of privacy?

- The European Union plans to replace national currencies with a single one as early as 1999 or, if delayed, A.D. 2002 (Revelation 13:7).

- Signs in the heavens: Scientists are puzzled over the strangest atmospheric discovery since cosmic rays. They are called "sprites"—blood-red apparitions with bluish tentacles that flash above the earth, sometimes near the edge of space. We had better become accustomed to these reports, because they will continue from now until Jesus comes.

- Scientists say a solar storm with a wave of destructive force to disrupt power lines, communication, and radar is projected to hit earth around January A.D. 2000. Called "the storm of the millennium," the billion-ton wave of super-hot electrically charged gas from the sun will smash into the earth's magnetic field at 620 miles per hour, according to a Scripps-Howard news report.

- *Intelligence Digest* reports that the Chechens may soon become the world's first nuclear-armed terrorists. They have the means, motive, and opportunity, reports the respected *British Journal*. Portable terrorism is just around the corner. No security measures will be able fully to eliminate the threat.

- The Russians have achieved one of their principle strategic goals of the cold war period—military cooperation with the Republic of South Africa. An agreement between Moscow and Nelson Mandela's government was quietly announced recently. Russia's sabers are again rattling. Not only is there now a friendly link with South Africa, but there's also a new, albeit delicate, détente with China. There is major trouble on that front. The cold war may be upon us once again.

- Egypt is moving further from its moderate, pro-Western stance and closer to harmony with the rising tide of Islamic fundamentalism Note this editorial in a recent edition of the nation's *Rose al-Yusaf* newspaper: "Hatred of the United States is no longer the prerogative of the crazies. It now extends to the sane. The American dream blinded the Egyptians for twenty years. Now it has turned into a macabre nightmare. The disgust of the Egyptian people with everything American is mounting."

## THE DOLLAR'S DEMISE

IF WE DO NOT read, study, and work to understand the events of the past, we will be doomed to repeat them. So it's important not only to quote current reports, but also those studies of years gone by. In that regard, there has never been a lack of economic experts in the United States to warn us that America's monetary system is in grave danger. Let's step back for a moment in history and review the thinking of people almost two decades ago.

In January of 1978, the United States intervened on a massive scale to bolster the dollar abroad by announcing an arrangement to back the battered currency through a $20 billion swap with foreign central banks, and through a special $4.7 billion currency stabilization fund. Previously, in order to strengthen the sagging dollar, Japan and West Germany had come to the rescue. When they refused to do so again, the U.S. Treasury and Federal Reserve System had to trade the more stable foreign currency on hand to purchase foreign-held U.S. dollars.

As we move closer to the year 2000, we discover that the United States will assuredly be forced to use its remaining gold to buy back Eurodollars and Petrodollars. When the last of this gold has been used to prop up these dollars, the day of the dollar will be finished and a new system will become necessary.

Another thorn in America's economic side is the billions of dollars we have loaned to Russia. Over the

> Another thorn in America's economic side is the billions of dollars we have loaned to Russia.

years, communist nations have borrowed in excess of one trillion dollars from the United States. If they default or refuse to repay these loans (which has already happened—or the loans have been forgiven,) we are finished, economically. In fact, economic articles written by the experts are, for the first time, in agreement on the possibility that the dollar could become obsolete. Leonard K. Ruse, president of the St. Louis

Federal Reserve Bank, stated in the *Journal of Commerce*, "The American economy may finally be running out of steam."

Again, looking to past history, Douglas R. Casey, in a *Detroit News* article written almost two decades ago, said, "The United States, in fact the entire world, now faces a massive depression. The effects . . . will persist well into and even beyond the 1980s and '90s. As wonderful as recent technological advances have been they will not postpone the inevitable. . . . Nor will the government."

In *International Money Line*, Julian Snyder says, "The U.S. is trying to solve its problems through currency depreciation. It never worked throughout history and will not work now." Meanwhile, the *Holt Investment Advisory* reports, "The efforts of government to solve problems by printing more paper money are making things worse. This is adding to the worldwide mistrust in paper money and strengthening the demand for gold."

As disheartening and bewildering as all this is, read this analysis and weep: *The Commercial Appeal* of Memphis, Tennessee, looked at the future and stated,

> "The average worker retiring at age sixty-five in 2050 would draw retirement checks of nearly $259,000 while some individuals would get the maximum of $405,000. If the Social Security projections hold true, wages will increase roughly sixty-two-fold over the next seventy-two years. If prices followed suit, today's sixty-cent loaf of bread would cost $37.50; a $25 tab at the grocery store would run $1,562; a fifteen-cent phone call or newspaper would cost $9.40; a medium-sized $4,500 auto would retail for $281,000; a $55,000 home would sell for $3.4 million, and that average $656,000 wage earner would be paying more than $50,000 annually in Social Security taxes. The maximum tax would be $114,000 on income up to $1.5 million."

I believe the *Commercial Appeal's* predictions will become reality long before 2050. If the Lord Jesus Christ tarries, I believe we will see such hyperinflation sweep our nation and the world within the next ten years. Many economic experts believe that financial destruction is just ahead of us. Meanwhile, in order to replace the downgraded dollar, the nations of the European Economic Community have created a new currency, the ECU, which fulfills both the role of international denominator and world reserve tender, the two key functions previously reserved for the dollar.

The ECU will be backed in gold and hard-currency reserves by the strongest European nations and firmly insulated against any fluctuations or disturbances caused by the instability of the dollar. To further eliminate U.S. economic leadership and the influence of dollar transactions, the European nations have agreed to replace the American-dominated International Monetary Fund with a European Monetary Fund endowed with billions of dollars in liquid assets. Under the control of this new anti-dollar money union, European currencies will be stabilized without—in fact, against—a U.S. presence.

The international bankers indeed have a plan. According to *The Fact Finder* of Phoenix, Arizona, and I paraphrase, the international bankers, most of whom reside in the United States, have limited loyalty to America, and certainly have no patriotism for the United States. Their essential aim is to alter our monetary system to make it easier for them to control all monetary systems, worldwide. What I have just reported may be one of the most important segments in this book. Because it will ultimately play into the "three numbers" which one day will be required to engage in any form of trade or commerce.

## SHADOWS OF "666"

A WORLD RULER must arise and work with this new monetary system in place. This beast is described in Revelation 13:7, 8, 16 and 17: "Power was given him over all kindreds, and tongues and nations. And all that dwell upon the earth shall worship him. . . . And he causeth all, both small and great, rich and poor, free and bond, to receive a mark in their right hand, or in their foreheads: And that no man might buy or sell, save he that had the mark, or the name of the beast, or the number of his name."

We addressed the issue of the number "666" in chapter 7. However, that survey was only a glimpse of what is really going on. Over the years, I have watched with awe the increasing use of "666" throughout the world. At first, many scoffed, saying, "What does Dr. Van Impe think he's doing, anyway? He's sure an alarmist. All this '666' talk. He's talking through his hat!" I find it interesting that I'm not hearing that criticism very much anymore.

> A world ruler must arise and work with this new monetary system in place.

Take the Middle East, for example. The proliferation of this number since its initial assignment to all Arab-owned vehicles in Jerusalem in 1973 is astounding. Is no one in that part of the world reading prophecy? Can it be that even Orthodox Jewish leaders are undeniably naive, and unaware of what is happening under their noses?

I'm now certain that the nations of the world are currently being brainwashed into accepting this code as normal and necessary to pave the way for its becoming an absolute requirement during the reign of the Antichrist. If you think such concerns cannot be backed up with concrete evidence, then I encourage you to quickly read the following list of thirty-three different places the number "666" has either shown up in the past, or is currently appearing. It is a number that's been in vogue and will continue to be used until its ultimate purpose will come to pass.

- The Hollywood film productions, *The Omen I* and *II* plus *The Final Conflict* were about the world dictator. The number "666" appeared in the advertisements for these movies.

- In 1973, the license plate numbers of all Arab-owned vehicles in the city of Jerusalem had been prefixed with "666."

- The first ship to pass through the reopened Suez Canal in 1975 displayed "666" on its side.

- Beginning in 1977, the IRS Circular E (supplement) Employer's Tax Guide W-2P form required a "666" prefix.

- Beginning in 1979, the IRS W-2 form for nonprofit corporation employees required the "666" prefix. (Note: I understand the IRS is changing its requirements as a result of public pressure.)

- The IRS Alcohol, Tobacco, and Firearms Division employee badges originally displayed the number "666."

- Metric rulers distributed throughout America in 1979 contained the number "666."

- The design of Australia's national bank card incorporates a configuration of the number "666."

- Shoes produced in Italy displayed a "666" label.

- An introduction-to-algebra book for children, released by the Thomas Crowell Company, New York, was titled *666 Jellybeans.*

- South Central Bell Telephone Company's Telco Credit Union card required a "666" prefix plus the holder's Social Security number at one time.

- Parent/teacher training books offered by the Channing L. Bete Co., Inc., Greenfield, Massachusetts, were catalog coded "C-666."

- Central computers for Sears, Belks, J.C. Penney, and Montgomery Ward stores around the world have variously used prefix transactions with "666."

- Numerous computer receipts across the U.S. have contained a "666" number.

- The formula for the NCR Model 304 supermarket computer was 6-06-6 or "666."

- Selective Service cards at one time contained a "666" code.

- Financial institutions in Florida have used the "666" number.

- The overseas telephone operator number from Israel was "666."

- Israel's national lottery tickets and advertisements prominently featured the number "666."

- The federal government's Medicaid service employees' division number has used "666."

- Some state governments have used "666" on paperwork for office purchases.

- The Koehring and Clark equipment companies have used "666" as part of their product identification on certain models.

- Armstrong "Sundial" has had a floor tile coded "666-13."

- Shirts produced in mainland China at one time contained a "666" label.

- Work gloves manufactured by the Boss Glove Company have prominently displayed the number "666."

- Crow's Hybrid Corn Company of Nevada, Iowa, once developed a "666" hybrid.

- The McGregor Clothing Company has advertised a "666 Collection" for men.

- The IBM equipment in America's supermarkets has displayed the number "3X666."

- The identification tags on Japanese parts received by the Caterpillar Company, Peoria, Illinois, contained the number "666."

- Stickers distributed at DuPont Company plants have stated, "To be in the know, call 'Mom' (666)."

- Materials produced by the Bliss-Hastings Company have used the number "666."

- "Performer Q," a little-known, semi-secret list of show business personalities used by programmers, productions studios, advertising agencies and others, allegedly contain the names of 666 individuals.

- More than fifteen years ago, the Eighty-fifth Annual Frontier Days Festival in Cheyenne, Wyoming, featured July 23, 1981, as "666 Rodeo Day."

As if the foregoing were not sufficient evidence that a brain-washing movement—perhaps even unknowingly designed to acquaint the public with the "new system"—is in progress, there are also full-page advertisements featuring the picture of a man with a Universal Product Code imprinted on his forehead. Whether or not the advertiser's "creative director" was privy to the prophetic implications of this ad is a moot point. One day soon, all buyers and sellers—the consumer and the producer alike—will be required to receive a mark in their right hand, or in their foreheads (Revelation 13:16). This requirement can only be initiated and enforced by the Antichrist himself!

> Antichrist cannot reign until the Holy Spirit's restraining influence is removed.

I believe that when the Antichrist makes his debut and officially institutes the number "666" internationally, we Christians will be gone. Paul makes this point emphatically clear in 2 Thessalonians 2:2–8. In verses 6–8, he informs the saints that the Antichrist cannot mount his throne until the hinderer—the Holy Spirit—is removed: "And now ye know what withholdeth [or what holds back the Antichrist's coming to power] that he might be revealed in his time. . . . only he who now letteth [hindereth] will let [hinder], until he be taken out of the way."

After the Restrainer's removal, then the wicked one will be revealed. Antichrist cannot reign until the Holy Spirit's restraining influence is removed. This restraining influence consists of believers in whose hearts the Spirit dwells. Christ must come to call His own out of this world before the leader of the one-world government assumes power.

## CLOSING OUT WORLD HISTORY

REMEMBER THAT the signs in God's Word point to Christ's return to the earth—when He comes as King of kings and Lord of lords. As you have seen in the preceding chapters, virtually every sign in the Bible indicates that Christians will be coming back soon with Jesus. But we can't do it at this time because we are still here on earth.

World events declare that Jesus Christ is coming soon. Never before in history have we had a confederacy of Western nations. Never in twenty-five centuries has there been an Israel that could sign a world peace contract with the one who comes to power, whoever he is and whenever it is. The signs are with us. John F. Walvoord, former president of Dallas Theological Seminary, has said,

> "From the hour that this world leader signs the peace contract with Israel, one can count down on the calendar seven years to the day—to the return of Christ as King."

"And he shall confirm the covenant with many for one week: and in the midst of the week he shall cause the sacrifice and oblation to cease, and . . . that determined shall be poured upon the desolate" (Daniel 9:27). Although he will sign a peace contract of seven years (or eighty-four months) duration, he will break it at the halfway point (forty-two months). Then Russia will march to the Middle East, for she says, "I will go up to the land of unwalled villages; I will go to them that are at rest that dwell safely . . ." (Ezekiel 38:11).

The clock is ticking. The end of time as we know it is fast approaching. The signs are everywhere—even in the heavens.

## DEBATE ABOUT THE AGE OF THE UNIVERSE

WE ALL GREW UP with the story of Chicken Little and the now-famous cry: "The sky is falling, the sky is falling!" When we became adults we all laughed at this innocent story, didn't we? How on earth could the sky fall? Chicken Little, as it turned out, was little more than a feathered alarmist! Well, maybe not.

While today the sky may not be literally falling, what is happening in the sky and in our environment as a whole should be a major concern to us. But before we launch into our discussion of the acceleration of climatic changes, and the appearance of new, and constantly changing phenomena in the heavens, let's look at the hot debate going on among scientists about the age of the universe. Their conclusions are beginning to approximate the counsel of the Word of God.

The more scientists learn about the age of the universe, the more confused they become. Using data obtained from the Hubble Space Telescope, astronomers at the University of California and the University of Washington have determined that the universe is thirteen billion years old.

Not only is this new finding flatly contradicted with the Bible, it is also in direct conflict with the scientists' own research which shows some stars to be sixteen billion years old. One news account concluded that the report feeds a rising suspicion that something is seriously amiss in cosmology, the study of the history of the universe.

**Could the universe be much younger than cosmologists believe?**

That's true. Until a short time ago, most cosmologists believed the universe was twenty billion years old. A group of astronomers led by Michael Pierce of Indiana University, however, concluded recently that it could be no older than seven billion years. Clearly, our best scientific minds have already been off in their calculations by three billion, six billion, or thirteen billion years. Could they be off even further? Could the universe indeed be much younger even than seven billion years?

The answer is unequivocally "yes." The Bible tells us that the universe was created on the first of seven days of creation. The stars and other heavenly bodies are much younger than today's scientists believe (see Genesis 1, 2). As scientists' theories about the heavens are shaken by new research, the earth itself continues to experience unprecedented tremors.

## THE AGE OF KILLER QUAKES AND VOLCANOES

FUTURIST GORDON-MICHAEL Scallion, editor of *Earth Changes Report,* has been suggesting for months that a frightening global killer earthquake pattern is emerging. He is predicting that a series of magnitude 10.0 quakes will rip up America's West Coast in the next few years.

As an indicator of whether his theory was correct, Scallion urged people to keep an eye on two dominant volcanoes in Europe—Mount Etna and Mount Vesuvius. In the weeks following Scallion's warning, volcano experts in Italy began predicting a major eruption of Mount Vesuvius similar to the one that destroyed the ancient city of Pompeii nearly two thousand years ago. Now scientists in the United States say the West Coast's Mount St. Helens is also ready to blow again. (See Matthew 24:7; Mark 13:8; Revelation 6:12, 8:5, 11:13, 16:18).

## QUAKES IN ASIA . . . TORNADOES IN CALIFORNIA

IT'S SOBERING to realize that never before in history have we witnessed so many killer quakes in such a short period of time. Two magnitude 7.0 quakes—one considered an extremely rare phenomenon—struck Indonesia and China within three weeks of each other, both resulting in major loss of life. The China quake struck the southwest part of the country on February 4,

1996, killing at least one hundred fifty people. The Indonesia quake struck the eastern part of the country on February 18, just two weeks later, killing more than fifty people. Such major quakes have been on the rise worldwide throughout the last two decades. Luke 21:11 reminds us, "And great earthquakes shall be in divers places, and famines, and pestilences; and fearful sights and great signs shall there be from heaven."

> **Scientists say Mount St. Helens is ready to blow again.**

And as if California didn't have enough natural disasters to worry about—with earthquakes, brushfires, mud slides, and floods—now comes word of a dramatic increase in tornadoes throughout the state. Sixty-three tornadoes were reported across the state in the last five years. That is more than double the incidence of tornadoes during the previous decade, which, in turn, was much higher than the decade before. In other words, from the 1950s, when records were first kept on such reports, tornadoes have increased in both frequency and intensity in California, a state previously not associated with such phenomena.

"And there shall be signs in the sun, and in the moon, and in the stars; and upon the earth distress of nations, with perplexity; the sea and the waves roaring" (Luke 21:25). The signs of the end times are before us as never before. The distress of humanity is mounting. The roaring of the sea and the violent movement of earth's tectonic plates are now ever-present. And the shaking and uncertainty goes well beyond terra firma. We're also seeing more signs in the sky—just as Jesus predicted two thousand years ago, and added, "When you see these things come to pass, know the Kingdom is nigh [close] at hand."

## STRANGE APPEARANCES IN THE HEAVENS OVER ISRAEL

THE JEWISH STATE is reporting a spate of UFO sightings, strange terrestrial occurrences such as cattle mutilations, close encounters of the third kind and, yes, even alien abductions.

More puzzling, say those who study such phenomena, is that the sightings appear to be occurring almost exclusively over the tiny land mass of the Jewish state rather than throughout the Middle East, as one might expect.

The respected *Jerusalem Report* magazine recently featured an article focusing on the case of Herzl Ksantini, a successful forty-two-year-old Israeli businessman, who last year reported coming face-to-face with a nine-foot-tall, mud-colored humanoid monster. While security agents found no monster after scouring the area, they did track deep footprints for some eight kilometers. Ksantini is only one of hundreds of Israelis who have reported experiences some believe to be unearthly. "Israel is recognized as an international UFO hot spot with an unsurpassed quantity and quality of evidence," says Barry Chamish, an American-born Israeli who studies the phenomena.

> We're also seeing more signs in the sky. . . .

A 1993 incident also involved some trace physical evidence—crop circles. Some presume these indicate spacecraft landings, in nearby gardens. Another dramatic incident was reported in the Jewish state back in 1987, accompanied by a month-long series of sightings over Haifa. The phenomena ended with a spectacular explosion that scorched the Shikmonah beach in the shape of a spacecraft. Tens of thousands came to witness the burn zone, which was highly magnetic and contained high concentrations of zinc. More recently, a woman from the community of Acre reported being visited by aliens who warned against the ongoing peace process with Arab neighbors.

But why all this activity over Israel and not in neighboring Arab countries? Some believe the answer is spiritual. Some suggest the angels of the Bible, who sometimes visited earth on "chariots of fire," (2 Kings 2:11; Ezekiel 7) are returning to herald the dawning of a new millennium. Others say the phenomena are part of a great deception perpetrated by demonic beings pretending to be from other planets and civilizations.

The idea that the operators of UFOs might be other than aliens from another world is being supported by some top-notch secular researchers. Some witnesses thought that they had seen demons because the creatures had the unpredictability and mischievousness associated with popular conceptions of the devil, writes Jacques Vallee, an astrophysicist and computer scientist and author of *Dimensions: A Casebook of Alien Contact.*

## ATHEISTS CHANGING THEIR TUNES

WHITLEY STRIEBER, author of the best-selling books *Communion* and *Transformation,* says this about his own encounter with an alien creature:

> "Increasingly I felt as if I were entering a struggle for my soul, my essence, or whatever part of me might have reference to the eternal. . . . I felt an absolutely indescribable sense of menace. It was hell on earth to be there. I couldn't move, cry out, and couldn't get away. I lay as still as death, suffering inner agonies. Whatever was there seemed so monstrously ugly, so filthy and dark and sinister. Of course they were demons. They had to be. . . ."

Whatever they are—aliens, angels, or demons—the appearance of these signs in the heavens over the holy land is beginning the fulfillment of Jesus' prophecy about terrors and great signs from heaven (or outer space) in the last days. The Greek word for "sign" literally means a supernatural phenomenon intended to point the observer to some profound truth. And there is no greater truth than the reality of Jesus' Second Coming.

Hear the Word of the Lord from Revelation 9:1–6:

> "And the fifth angel sounded, and I saw a star fall from heaven unto the earth: and to him was given the key of the

bottomless pit. And he opened the bottomless pit; and there arose a smoke out of the pit, as the smoke of a great furnace; and the sun and the air were darkened by reason of the smoke of the pit. And there came out of the smoke locusts upon the earth: and unto them was given power, as the scorpions of the earth have power. And it was commanded them that they should not hurt the grass of the earth, neither any green thing, neither any tree; but only those men which have not the seal of God in their foreheads. And to them it was given that they should not kill them, but that they should be tormented five months: and their torment was as the torment of a scorpion, when he striketh a man. And in those days shall men seek death, and shall not find it; and shall desire to die, and death shall flee from them."

## HOW ISLAM ATTACKS THE CHURCH

ALTHOUGH SOME may find that death will flee from them, for many others in today's world, death is all too real. For countless Christians around the globe, death comes at the hands of those who hate the living God, who oppose the work of His Son, and decry the faith of His people. One of the signs of the end is an increase in the persecution of believers throughout the world. As you read the following accounts, I urge you to say a prayer for those who are being abused, persecuted, and even killed for their faith throughout the world.

> One of the signs of the end is an increase in the persecution of believers. . . .

John 16:1–3 prophesies . . . "These things have I spoken unto you, that ye should not be offended. They shall put you out of the synagogues: yea, the time cometh, that whosoever killeth you will think that he doeth God service. And these things will they do unto you, because they have not known the Father, nor me."

I almost shake when I read this prophecy, especially with our newspapers and television reports filled with stories of an increased Middle East-sponsored terrorism that commits its dastardly deeds against "infidels" (read *Jews and Christians*) with the promise that because they are doing God's service, by killing these enemies, their places in heaven will be fully assured. Heightened by this rise in international terrorism, Islamic fundamentalism, and a global ethic of secular humanism, Christians are facing persecution worldwide in unprecedented numbers—just as the Bible predicted for the time before Jesus returns to Earth.

Pope John Paul II recognizes this trend, and recently issued a stern and forthright call on the Muslim world to extend full freedom of worship to Christians. Unfortunately, his pleas received scant media attention in the West. Nor have the growing horrors faced by believers suffering under Islamic oppression and atheistic totalitarian rule around the world been widely reported.

The Pope made his remarks the day that Europe's largest Islamic mosque was dedicated in Rome, just a few miles northeast of Vatican City, seat of the Roman Catholic Church. He said: "It is significant that in Rome, the center of Christianity and the seat of St. Peter's successor, Muslims should have their own place of worship with full respect for their freedom of conscience.

"On a significant occasion like this, it is unfortunately necessary to point out that in some Islamic countries, similar signs of the recognition of religious freedom are lacking," Pope John Paul II continued. "And yet the world, on the threshold of the third millennium, is waiting for these signs."

## THE SUDAN: NEW CHRISTIAN KILLING FIELDS

WHAT IS THE POPE talking about? Let's take a look at what is happening in the Islamic nation of Sudan. According to new evidence gathered by a recent fact-finding mission, the Sudanese government is officially using slavery and other coercive measures to turn the ethnically and religiously diverse African nation into a unified Islamic state in the Iran model. The team was led by Britain's deputy speaker of the House of Lords, Baroness Caroline Cox, and Christian Solidarity International's John Eibner, both veteran Sudan observers. Here's some of what they heard from one community leader in the Nuba Mountains: "When [government] troops attack towns and villages, they try to kill as many Christians as possible and destroy churches as a matter of priority, leaving mosques intact."

At least three Protestant clergymen, Reverend Matta Nur, Reverend Matta Stepanous, and Reverend Harun Angelu, have been executed recently, the CSI team was told. Marauding troops burned down the Protestant churches in the villages of Dere and Abri, both in the southeastern quarter of the Nuba Mountains. The pastor of those churches, Reverend Isaac Ghanian, was captured, and his fate remains unknown, the community leaders reported.

In addition to attacks against churches and clergy, several young southern Christian boys and girls gave the team firsthand accounts of being taken as slaves, beaten or raped, and given Muslim names. Similar Islamic repression against believers is being reported throughout much of north Africa, central Asia, the Middle East, the Persian Gulf, Indonesia, the Philippines, and Southeast Asia. There seems to be no end in sight.

## CHINA'S WAR ON CHRISTIANITY

AFTER READING John 15:18–19, it should no longer come as a surprise that a violent, unbending persecution of believers will escalate at the end of the age. Christians will be hated, rebuffed, and destroyed in increasing numbers, even as the gospel predicts: "If the world hate you, ye know that it hated me before *it hated* you. If ye were of the world, the world would love his own: but because ye are not of the world, but I have chosen you out of the world, therefore the world hateth you."

However, it's not just in the Muslim world where persecution of believers is on the rise. China, the world's largest nation, seems hell-bent on a crusade to reduce organized Christianity to ashes. According to reliable church sources in Hong Kong, tensions between security officials and unregistered house church Christians in central and eastern China have escalated in recent months, with authorities in several provinces conducting mass arrests of church members for "illegal religious activities." The officials were reported to have used electric batons during the raids, injuring a number of those taken into custody.

According to Hong Kong's *South China Morning Post,* Public Security Bureau officials in the Henan city of Zhoukou have arrested and fined more than two hundred house church Christians since October 1994. A Chinese source who spoke to the *Post* said the latest police crackdown in Zhoukou occurred when authorities arrested fifty-eight Christians for conducting "illegal religious activities." The source said that more than forty are still being held in custody. In some cases, tensions have escalated so dramatically that congregations have stopped singing during services to avoid police detection.

Second Timothy 3:12–14 puts the impending persecution in black and white:

> "Yea, and all that will live godly in Christ Jesus shall suffer persecution. But evil men and seducers shall wax worse and worse, deceiving, and being deceived. But continue thou in the things which thou hast learned and hast been assured of, knowing of whom thou hast learned *them.*"

Revelation 13:5–7 makes it even clearer that war with the saints will be rampant, and that power will be given to those who oppress Christ's church:

> "And there was given unto him a mouth speaking great

things and blasphemies; and power was given unto him to continue forty *and* two months. And he opened his mouth in blasphemy against God, to blaspheme his name, and his tabernacle, and them that dwell in heaven. And it was given unto him to make war with the saints, and to overcome them: and power was given him over all kindreds, and tongues, and nations."

## PERSECUTION OF CHRISTIANS INCREASING WORLDWIDE

IN LAOS, all known Protestant and Catholic churches in the two northern Laotian provinces of Sayabuly and Luang Prabang have been forced to cease operations and close. This comes as part of a government campaign to coerce Laotian Christians into renouncing their faith, according to Laos church analysts. Since November 1994, government authorities have conducted seminars in many areas of the country in an effort to educate rural villagers about government and Communist Party policies regarding religion.

In Vietnam, a Vietnamese-American pastor and his Vietnamese-Canadian colleague were detained and held under house arrest for three days by police in the northern Vietnamese city of Haiphong for "meeting and worshipping in a restricted military area." The two Christians were later released from custody, after being fined and ordered to leave the country within ten days.

In Bosnia, almost 95 percent of Roman Catholics from the Serb-held city of Banja Luka have been forced to flee, according to local church sources. However, further expulsions have been temporarily halted in expectation of an offensive against the region by combined Croatian and Bosnian forces.

**Persecution of Christians is not limited to Muslim nations.**

In Algeria, two more Roman Catholic nuns were assassinated in early September 1995, bringing to ten the number of Catholic clerics and religious workers murdered in the North

African country since May 1994. According to Catholic sources, Sisters Bibiane, sixty-five, and Angele-Marie, sixty-two, were walking home from a vespers service in the Algiers district of Belcourt when they were both shot in the head by unknown assailants. And in May 1996, five Trappist monks had their throats slit by Algerian Islamic Terrorists. One of the murdered Trappists was eighty years old.

In Egypt, a Christian man from the Giza district of Cairo has alleged that Muslim neighbors abducted his seventeen-year-old daughter and forced her to convert to Islam. Coptic Christians in Egypt have long charged that the Arab world is funding a campaign to compensate Muslims who succeed in converting Christian youths to Islam. Yet few Christians have been willing to provide documentation about this sensitive issue.

In Pakistan, a fourteen-year-old Pakistani Christian school-girl converted to Islam less than two weeks after her Muslim teacher accused her of blasphemy. The girl's Muslim step-father, Shakeel Ullah Khan, said his stepdaughter, Carol Daphnie, had embraced Islam and taken the Muslim name of Aysha in order to quell social unrest in the Sindh Province city of Sukkur.

Again, the prophetic words of John 16:1–3 remind us of what is still to come as we come closer to 2001, the edge of eternity. . . . "These things have I spoken unto you, that ye should not be offended. They shall put you out of the synagogues: yea, the time cometh, that whosoever killeth you will think that he doeth God service. And these things will they do unto you, because they have not known the Father, nor me."

Doom and gloom, you say? Perhaps. But it all depends on your perspective. The bad news is that conflict and mayhem are the order of the day. Mass killings of Christians, summary executions of those who even inquire about the Christian faith, and human rights abuses across the board abound. All these are predicted in God's reliable Word. The good news is that you need not be discouraged, despondent, or depressed.

Everything you have read so far points to one wonderful, hopeful event—the near return of our Lord and Savior Jesus Christ.

Jesus said in Luke 21:9, 28, "When you shall hear of wars and commotions be not terrified for all these things must first come to pass. When you see these things come to pass, know that the Kingdom of God is nigh at hand."

As the clock ticks even faster now, be encouraged that the kingdom of God is indeed at hand.

## 9

## THE LATE, GREAT UNITED STATES AND THE COMING SHOWDOWN WITH RUSSIA

**Y**OU'VE READ THE REPORTS in newspapers across America:

- In America's inner cities, motorists sporting gold-plated custom car wheels are being murdered by thieves in search of the fancy $4,500 rims.

- A family takes a wrong turn into gang territory and faces automatic weapons fire that kills a three-year-old and injures a two-year-old.

- Multiplied murders in America's cities include decapitations (beheadings).

- Two FBI agents and a police sergeant are murdered in an attack inside police headquarters.

The United States is becoming a very dangerous place to live. In fact, according to the American Medical Association, some of the worst human rights abuses are taking place right inside America's families.

## ABUSE AND CRIME CONTINUE UNABATED

MORE THAN 70,000 women are sexually assaulted every year in the United States. That's one every forty-five seconds, making sexual assault the most rapidly growing violent crime in the country. Three-quarters of these assaults are committed by a friend, acquaintance, intimate partner, or family member of the victim.

Domestic violence is more widespread than ever. Each year between two and four million women are battered; 1,500 women are murdered by their intimate partners; 1.8 million elderly are victims of maltreatment; 1.7 million child abuse reports are filed each year.

**Our nation is awash in a tidal wave of violence that has reached epidemic proportions . . .**

All this abuse is expected to result in an explosive crime rate in the next few years when today's elementary-age children become tomorrow's adolescents. The experts say a youth-crime crisis is right around the corner. At the current growth rate there will be nearly a half-million more adolescent boys in the year 2010 than there are today. That trend would mean there will be 30,000 more chronic juvenile delinquents on the streets in fifteen years.

Though representing only 7 percent of all male teens, these chronic offenders commit 70 percent of all serious crime in their age group.

Our nation is awash in a tidal wave of violence that has reached epidemic proportions, especially among the youngest generation. Faith in the criminal justice system to punish the guilty and protect the innocent has eroded even further since the O. J. Simpson trial. One distinguished British journalist, after observing the jury in the case, said "the thought that one day such individuals might actually decide your fate, will, if you are innocent, fill you with absolute terror."

## FEAR, FEAR, AND MORE FEAR

IN AMERICA'S URBAN centers, fear is everywhere. People are fleeing their homes and neighborhoods, their jobs, and their friends to get away from preteen pregnancies, free condom distributors in public schools, drive-by shootings, kiddie pornographers, abortion-on-demand advocates, suicide machines, and child abusers.

Since 1960 there has been a 560 percent increase in violent crime. In the last thirty years, illegitimate births have increased 419 percent. Divorce rates have tripled. The number of children living in single-parent homes has tripled. The teen suicide rate has increased 200 percent.

As bad as it is, these events should surprise no one familiar with Bible prophecy. God's Word explains in great detail how badly conditions on earth will deteriorate in the days just before Jesus returns. Second Timothy 3:1–7 reminds,

> "This know also, that in the last days perilous times shall come. For men shall be lovers of their own selves, covetous, boasters, proud, blasphemers, disobedient to parents, unthankful, unholy, Without natural affection, trucebreakers, false accusers, incontinent, fierce, despisers of those that are good, Traitors, heady, highminded, lovers of pleasures more than lovers of God; Having a form of godliness, but denying the power thereof: from such turn away. For of this sort are they which creep into houses, and lead captive silly women laden with sins, led away with divers lusts, ever learning, and never able to come to the knowledge of the truth."

Does this not sound like a portrait of the times in which we live? The bad news is that things are going to get worse. But, as we've stated so often, the good news is that Jesus is coming back.

### ALL TRUTH IS UNDER ATTACK

THERE'S A VIRTUAL "culture war" against the values of the Bible in the United States. While Christians are not yet being locked up for their beliefs in our country, they are being broadly discriminated against in the public square. Is it so difficult to imagine what the next phase might be? The traditional family is breaking down in record numbers. Marriages are dissolving at an unprecedented rate.

In the United States, strangers commit 53 percent of all homicides, according to the FBI. Only 12 percent of all murders take place within the family. Violent crime of all kinds is on the rise, and authorities seem helpless to get a handle on the situation. In the 1960's, the United States had 3.3 police officers for every violent crimes reported per year. In 1993, it had 3.47 violent crime reported for every police officer. Things are about to get worse—much worse.

In the past decade the most violent and crime-prone age group—fifteen to twenty-four—has been stagnating or declining. But here's what's alarming. Against all projections to the contrary, crime has been rising steadily, and now this is about to explode. By the year 2005, demographers say the population aged fourteen to seventeen will increase 23 percent. As a result, some say, there will be an epidemic of teenage crime with 35,000 to 40,000 teenage homicides a year in the United States.

Surely this is the time of which Jesus spoke in Matthew 24:12, ". . . because iniquity shall abound, the love of many shall wax cold."

This sounds unmistakably like the late-1990s to me. More importantly, the signs of Jesus' return to earth are coming together as never before. There's a convergence of prophetic fulfillment on all fronts, and it all will affect—or is already affecting—life as we've come to know it:

• Changing weather patterns (Luke 21:25)

- Jerusalem emerging as an international bone of contention (Zechariah 12:2, 3)

- The resumption of Temple rituals in Israel (Daniel 9:27; Matthew 24:1–5; and 2 Thessalonians 2:2, 4)

- The rise of fervently anti-Israel Islamic fundamentalism (Psalm 83:4)

- Russia's new militancy and adventurism and its alliance with the Islamic world (Ezekiel 38:2–6)

- The emergence of a world military power in Asia (Revelation 16:12)

- The rise of a united Europe (Daniel 2 and 7; Revelation 12:3; 13:1)

Time is growing short. As we approach the third millennium, I encourage you to be alert to the agenda of the globalists—those who would subvert our national sovereignty and our birthright as Americans in favor of a few misguided United Nations proposals. It's happening already, but look for the trend to accelerate in the days ahead as the one-worlders become bolder, and increasingly desperate. Disease, drought, famine, conflict, pollution, and natural disasters—these, sadly, will be the order of the day for the next few years. Many will occur here in the United States.

> "And when these things begin to come to pass, then look up, and lift up your heads; for your redemption draweth nigh."
> —Luke 21:28

But don't be discouraged, and don't become alarmed. All of what is happening in our nation points to one very hopeful event—the imminent return of Jesus Christ. The Saviour said in Luke 21:9, "When you shall hear of wars and commotions be not terrified for all these things must first come to pass." He adds in verse 28: "And when these things begin to come to pass, then look up, and lift up your heads; for your redemption draweth nigh."

## AIDS ON THE INCREASE IN U.S.

AN AIDS STRAIN linked to the explosive heterosexual epidemics in Asia and Africa was discovered for the first time in the United States in five young servicemen routinely tested in California.

In some parts of Tanzania, one in four mothers is HIV-positive. Of the country's twenty-six million people, an estimated 1.2 million are already infected. When will we be reporting similar numbers in the United States? At our present rate of infection, it may not be in the too distant future.

Experts fear that if this foreign strain of AIDS gains a toe-hold in America, the pattern of AIDS transmission may change, spreading much more among heterosexual men and women. The AIDS-B virus found in the Western world has infected about 1.5 million people, primarily homosexuals and intravenous drug users.

In Asia and Africa, however, subtypes E, C, D, and A have infected about twenty million heterosexual men, women, and children and are spreading fast. Some experts fear that if these foreign strains continue to spread at their current rate, 110 million adults and some ten million children would be infected by the year 2000.

What does God's Word say about this epidemic of terror and despair? Revelation 6:8–9 tells it like it is going to be in the end times. These verses prophesied the events long before they came to pass. . . .

> "And I looked and behold a pale horse: and his name that sat on him was Death, and Hell followed with him. And power was given unto them over the fourth part of the earth, to kill with the sword, and with hunger, and with death, and with the beasts of the earth. And when he had opened the fifth seal, I saw under the altar the souls of them that were slain for the word of God, and for the testimony which they held."

A top American AIDS researcher warns that virulent strains of HIV responsible for explosive foreign outbreaks among heterosexuals are headed to the United States. Dr. Max Essex, chairman of the Harvard AIDS Institute, sees more than a 50-50 chance for a major outbreak of the kind that has plagued Africa and other areas of the world before the end of the first decade of the next millennium.

A Utah man was diagnosed with AIDS but tested negative for HIV. This is a frightening development for AIDS researchers because it makes reliable testing and screening much more difficult.

## CHILD ABUSE ON THE RAMPAGE IN U.S.

ONE OF THE MOST terrible files in my possession is getting thicker every day. It's simply labeled Child Abuse in the United States. This is hardly a pleasant litany of statistics, but it's important that we know what is really happening. Because the following data is yet another prime indicator that we may well be on our last legs as a nation:

- More than three million children are physically abused every year in the United States.

- Nearly 5 percent of parents questioned in a recent survey admitted punishing children by punching, kicking, throwing the child down, or hitting the child with a hard object somewhere other than the bottom.

- A Gallup poll found 1.3 million kids are sexually abused each year.

- When it comes to child abuse (physical or sexual), parents are the primary culprits.

- Researchers estimate that day-care centers are 30 percent to 60 percent safer for children than their own homes.

- The real extent of the problem of child sexual abuse is unknown because all statistics are based on disclosures, and most experts feel that no more than one in nine incidents is disclosed.

- Statistics show that there is no difference between churchgoers and those who say they have no church affiliation regarding the percentage of abusers.

- Most cases of sexual abuse (80 percent) occur within the context of the family, and the typical abuser is an authoritative adult male whose children fear him.

### DRUGS ARE BACK: A PLAGUE ON ALL OUR HOUSES

AFTER DECLINING steadily through the 1980s, drug use, especially by teenagers, is making a big comeback. This is the view of law enforcement authorities in the United States and around the world. In the U.S., daily marijuana use has quadrupled among eighth-graders since 1992, according to a University of Michigan study.

**Drug use . . . is making a big comeback.**

Half of high school seniors say they have used illegal drugs at least once. Inhalants—breathable chemical vapors from common household products that produce psychoactive effects—are another popular form of substance abuse. LSD and PCP, powerful hallucinogens, are now more popular than ever. Rohypnol, or "roofie," a sedative stronger than valium, is another hot drug

The use of MDMA, or "ecstasy," which produces feelings of euphoria, is on the rise. And even heroin, cocaine, and "speed" are being used regularly again by kids as young as twelve. And I don't need to tell you that drugs are no respecter of neighborhoods. They are everywhere. You can run, but neither you nor your family can hide from their pernicious influence. As we approach the end of the age, drugs will proliferate. It will continue to get worse before it gets better.

Why the increase? Experts say that for thirteen years, drug use plummeted because of an unrelenting and unified chorus of objection in the schools, in the media, and by government and social leaders. The skyrocketing usage seems to have paralleled the apparent reduced concern with this problem. Worse, there is an undeniable relationship between crime and drugs.

Drug use lowers inhibitions among offenders and spurs them on to other crimes to finance their dependency. Therefore, the increased use of drugs by young people is one of the reasons experts are predicting an unprecedented surge in youth crime during the next decade.

What does the Bible have to say about this trend? In Revelation 9:21 we learn, "Neither repented they of their murders, nor of their sorceries, nor of their fornication, nor of their thefts."

I want you to look carefully at that word *sorceries*. Because the prophets say that at the hour just before the return of Jesus, all the nations of the world will be hooked on drugs. One of the names used in the Bible to describe this plague is *sorcery*, coming from the Greek root word *pharmakeia*, which is also the word from which we derive the English word "pharmacy." Not since the 1960s have we seen such a pattern developing.

In Revelation 18:23, this *sorcery* is confirmed, "And the light of a candle shall shine no more at all in thee; and the voice of the bridegroom and of the bride shall be heard no more at all in thee: for thy merchants were the great men of the earth; for by thy sorceries were all nations deceived."

Not since Jesus ascended into heaven nearly two thousand years ago have the prophecies of the Bible been fulfilled before our eyes on such a grand scale.

## ISLAMIC TERROR IN THE UNITED STATES?

WITH FRIENDS in high places, an infrastructure for Islamic terrorism is being built right under your nose and mine. Many in the United States were shocked when Nation of Islam leader

Louis Farrakhan, on a nine-nation tour of Middle Eastern and African Islamic states, accepted a pledge of one billion dollars from Libya's Moammar Ghadafy "to unify Muslims in America." Libya, of course, is one of the principal exporters of terrorism in the world. And Farrakhan, despite his record of openly racist and anti-Semitic rhetoric, recently demonstrated his popular appeal among African-Americans by rallying hundreds of thousands in the nation's capital.

No one should be surprised by Farrakhan's trip, which also took him to Iran, Iraq, and Syria, three other international supporters of Islamic terrorism. As early as 1985, Farrakhan visited Ghadafy and reportedly collected a five-million-dollar loan to assist Nation of Islam "business projects." That same year, at a convention in Chicago, Ghadafy told Nation of Islam followers via satellite that he wanted to help sponsor an armed black revolution in America.

Even earlier, Farrakhan traveled to Uganda, where he had nothing but praise for its cannibalistic ruler Idi Amin, responsible for the murders of thousands of his own countrymen. In 1983, Farrakhan accompanied Jesse Jackson to Syria shortly after Jackson became a candidate for president. Farrakhan warned at the time that if Jackson did not win, a race war would ensue. His closest aide, Khalid Abdul Mohammed, told a group of college students that year that Jews were "blood-suckers" and that blacks should kill all the whites in South Africa. However, it wasn't until his successful "Million-Man March" on Washington that Farrakhan was really taken seriously by the international Islamic terror machine.

> Islamic terrorism is no longer limited to Middle Eastern soil.

"Our confrontation with America was like a fight against a fortress from outside, and today we found a breach to enter into this fortress and confront it," Ghadafy was quoted by his official news agency Jana. "On this basis, we agreed with Louis Farrakhan and his delegation to mobilize in a legal and legitimate form the oppressed minorities and at their forefront the blacks, Arab Muslims, and Red Indians, for they play an important role in American political life and have a weight in U.S. elections." In another Jana story, the two leaders said they agreed to fight America from the inside.

Does such treachery not indicate that the title of this chapter, "The Late, Great United States," may not be hyperbole at all, but rather accurate reporting on events present and yet to come?

Before Farrakhan left Iran for Syria, a Tehran newspaper quoted him as saying Allah would give the Muslims "the honor of bringing America down." In Iraq, Farrakhan met with Saddam Hussein and called on the U.S. to "halt its mass murder of Iraqis." While the U.S. State Department investigated the legality of Farrakhan's trip, international intelligence analysts were still trying to figure out just what his intentions and capabilities were—especially with a one-billion-dollar gift from Ghadafy.

"Terrorist war is the only kind Ghadafy and Farrakhan can wage in America," observed a veteran foreign affairs expert. Because we are truly a global community now—when one nation gets a cold, and a country half-way around the world sneezes—whatever happens on the foreign front will have ramifications for us at home.

In that context, what this analyst says about Ghadafy's other exploits becomes even more significant. He went on, ". . . Ghadafy attempted to improve relations with Britain by giving details on the extent to which he had helped arm and finance IRA (Irish Republican Army) terrorism over the past twenty years. He gave the names of twenty IRA terrorists trained in Libya camps, details on the some fourteen million dollars he had provided and the one hundred thirty tons of arms shipped to the IRA between 1985 and 1987. This, with the high-powered sniper-rifles supplied by sympathizers in the United States and unlimited supplies of semtex, was sufficient to make a relative number of gullible or determined IRA fighters see no reason why they should ever give up. It was Ghadafy's 'war on the inside' in Britain. Such a war in America will be infinitely worse."

Is such a war really thinkable or possible? Some say it has already begun. Besides the bombing of the World Trade Center in New York, a classified Pentagon study has concluded the Oklahoma City bombing of 1995 was caused, not by one bomb planted by suspect Timothy McVeigh, but five separate explosives with a "Middle East signature." McVeigh, the report suggests, was involved, but as a "useful idiot"—or scapegoat.

## WILL THE U.S. SOBER UP?

THERE MAY BE a reluctance to counter the Islamic terror threat for political reasons. For instance, President Clinton and his wife Hillary have repeatedly met with representatives of the American Muslim Council, an organization that supports the Palestinian terrorist group Hamas.

People who have put their lives on the line for peace without compromise—and who unequivocally condemn militant Islamic groups—feel betrayed by an administration that continually cozies up to such an extremist group.

The signs are everywhere. We are in the last days.

What does all this mean from a prophetic standpoint? America, the world's sole remaining superpower, does not seem to play a significant role in the end-time scenario as described by the prophets. Why? Some scholars suggest America will be severely weakened—even neutralized—by the time the critical events leading up to the Lord's return occur.

Economic collapse? Moral decay? Poor leadership? Nuclear attack? All are possibilities.

The signs are everywhere. We are in the last days. Two parallel developments are especially dramatic—the decline of the United States of America as a world leader and the increasing bellicosity and adventurism of Russia.

## HOME OF THE FREE: BUT FOR HOW LONG?

AMERICA IS STILL the greatest nation on the face of the earth. It has a proud tradition as a bulwark of liberty and freedom. As the child of Belgian immigrants, I still get choked up when I see the Statue of Liberty, when I pledge allegiance to the flag, or when I sing "America the Beautiful."

But let's remember, God has blessed America because it was founded as "one nation under God" and upon sound biblical principles. Today, righteousness has been debased, and Judeo-Christian values have been replaced by secular humanism. America has never been in such a state of degradation and hopelessness. Here are some facts to ponder about our own cultural decay:

- Ten million inebriates drink themselves into insensibility on a daily basis.

- Another ten million Americans are abusing drugs.

- Americans spend ten billion dollars a year polluting their bodies with tobacco products.

- Some sixty billion dollars a year is thrown away on gambling—both state-sanctioned lotteries as well as illegal betting.

- Sexual promiscuity is being condoned and even encouraged by government and judicial action.

- Pornography is a multi-billion-dollar industry.

- Millions of children are now born out of wedlock, many to girls as young as eleven.

- Abortion has taken the lives of twenty-five million unborn children since 1973.

- Euthanasia is the next big legal killing field, as states adopt laws permitting doctors to put patients asleep like animals.

- Murder now claims the lives of fifty thousand Americans a year.

- Cybersex on the Internet, and a proliferation of on-line pornography, bring XXX-rated material into millions of our homes where children are logging on to evil.

No nation can long survive under such sinful circumstances. The Bible says, "Righteousness exalteth a nation; but sin is a reproach to any people" (Proverbs 14:34).

Psalm 9:17 declares, "The wicked shall be turned into hell, and all the nations that forget God."

America has indeed forgotten God.

It's true that America is not mentioned in the Bible by name. However, it is written that "all nations" will suffer judgment in the days before the return of our Lord Jesus Christ (Micah 5:15; Ezekiel 39:2). Ezekiel 38:13 does single out Tarshish and all her "young lions," a group of nations that pays a heavy price for coming to the defense of Israel when it is invaded by Russia and a coalition of other nations. The name Tarshish is found twenty times in the Bible and always refers to the land farthest west of Israel. The text refers to the eleven merchants of Tarshish, and explains that these people trade goods around the world. Specifically, I believe Tarshish refers to Britain, and all of her "young lions" refers to the English-speaking world—including the United States.

Isaiah 18:1-2 issues a warning to a nation, "Woe to the land shadowing with wings, which *is* beyond the rivers of Ethiopia: that sendeth ambassadors by the sea, even in vessels of bulrushes upon the waters, *saying*, go ye swift messengers, to a nation scattered and peeled, to a people terrible from their beginning, hitherto; a nation meted out and trodden down, whose land the rivers have spoiled."

The nation described in this text is in dire difficulty with God because the opening word *woe* in the text is judgmental. This nation has the insignia of wings—similar to America's national emblem, the bald eagle. It is a land that is beyond the sea from Israel. This designation of "beyond Ethiopia," eliminates all of the nations of Europe, Asia, and Africa. It is a land scattered and peeled—meaning stretched out and having a large land mass. It is measured and staked out with its counties, cities, and states. It is a land with polluted rivers. Does this not sound unmistakably like the United States of America?

> **It's true that America is not mentioned in the Bible by name.**

In Jeremiah, chapters 50–51, the Holy Spirit talks about a nation called Babylon which is destroyed by an assembly of nations from the north. This is not a reference to ancient Babylon, which was attacked by the Medes and Persians. This Babylon, unlike most other nations, has "a mother." In a true sense, of course, America has a mother—Britain. This Babylon is the youngest among the great world powers of the day—as is America. It is a wealthy nation of mingled people—or a "melting pot," if you will. It is also a nation that dwells upon many waters. In Revelation, chapter 18, John the Apostle also alludes to this nation—a rich land laden with sins that has glorified herself and lived deliciously.

As I continue to read and study the prophetic writings of Scripture, I become more and more convinced that this is a direct reference to the United States. The present hedonistic pleasure-craze of our nation will not last forever. America's destruction may come as quick as lightning. We could indeed prove to be the battered and beaten Babylon of the following texts:

> "For, lo, I will raise and cause to come against Babylon an assembly of great nations from the north country: and they shall set themselves in array against her. . . ."
>
> —JEREMIAH 50:9

> "Alas, alas that great city Babylon, that mighty city! For in one hour is thy judgment come. . . ."
>
> —REVELATION 18:10

"Alas, Alas, that great city, that was clothed in fine linen, and purple, and scarlet, and decked with gold, and precious stones, and pearls! For in one hour so great riches is come to naught. And every shipmaster, and all the company in ships, and sailors, and as many as trade by sea, stood afar off, And cried when they saw the smoke other burning, saying, what city is like unto this great city! And they cast dust on their beads, and cried weeping and waiting, saying, Alas, alas that great city, wherein were made rich all that bad ships in the sea by reason of her costliness! for in one hour is she made desolate."

—REVELATION 18:16–19

As we near the twenty-first century, a nuclear attack in one hour's time could obliterate everything our nation took two centuries to build. And only in today's world could such vast destruction occur. Dr. Logsdon, former pastor of Moody Memorial Church in Chicago, propounded the U.S.A./Babylonian Theory and to this scholar and others, I am endebted. If God has America in mind—and it certainly appears that way—then what? Are you and your loved ones prepared for the judgment that may soon fall upon our nation without warning? This judgment will link the United States and Russia in a conflict to make the cold war appear to have been a walk in the park.

## UNITED STATES VS. RUSSIA:

EZEKIEL 38 and 39 show clearly that Russia—the biblical Magog—will attack Israel in the last days. The texts I have cited previously also strongly suggest that America will be victimized simultaneously by an all-out nuclear first strike by Russia.

I know we all continue to hear that the cold war is over and that Russia is disarming. We've been told that there is little or nothing for us to worry about any more. All is supposedly secure. We can now rest in peace, cut back on our defenses, and know with confidence that our erstwhile enemy, Russia, is no longer the "evil empire." Nonsense! As we've already discussed, Russia is more dangerous and unstable today than ever before. And relations between Washington and Moscow are worsening almost daily.

"I would say that indeed the honeymoon has come to an end," said Russian Foreign Minister Andrei Kozyrev in a Reuters dispatch on March 23, 1995, after two days of talks with U.S. Secretary of State Warren Christopher over major differences between the two world powers. The U.S. was protesting Russia's brutal invasion of Chechnya and its deal to help Iran build nuclear power plants that could be used to produce weapons-grade plutonium.

## WHAT HAPPENS AFTER THE HONEYMOON?

THE RUSSIANS MAY know the honeymoon is over, but it seems that most of our U.S. leaders still have their heads buried in the sand. Money is still flowing to Russia from the West. And while Russia is modernizing its nuclear arsenal, the U.S. is unilaterally disarming at an unprecedented rate. All the while, Russia remains undeniably deceptive in its dealings with the rest of the world. I don't believe the pronouncements of their leaders for a single moment, and neither should you.

Remember, it was Russian revolutionary V. I. Lenin who said his country would always be willing to take one step backward and two steps forward—feigning weakness, while aggressively pursuing its global objectives. Is there any question that Russia is still in the deception business?

An April 7, 1995 *Los Angeles Times* article revealed that Russian President Boris Yeltsin had broadened the powers of the successor agency of the KGB to allow searches without warrants, legalize electronic surveillance, and revive the gathering of foreign intelligence. That sounds a lot like what was happening during the cold war, does it not?

The situation in Russia worsens with each passing day: a loaf of bread costs 1,500 rubles—about 8 percent of some monthly salaries. The average prices for rent, heat, and electricity often increase as much as 250 percent in one month. The fee for public transportation has increased 2000 percent since 1994. And to make matters worse, workers are simply not being paid in some enterprises.

## IN THE MIDST OF TERROR—GOOD NEWS

BUT FOR THOSE OF US who are washed in the blood of the Lamb, and who have turned our lives over to the King of kings and Lord of lords, it will be a different story. As the plot leading to the end of time as we know it unravels, and as we move to the end of history and into the new millennium, we will be living out the prophesies of Isaiah 65:22–25:

> "They shall not build, and another inhabit; they shall not plant, and another eat: for as the days of a tree *are* the days of my people, and mine elect shall long enjoy the work of their hands. They shall not labour in vain, nor bring forth for trouble; for they *are* the seed of the blessed of the Lord, and their offspring with them. And it shall come to pass, that before they call, I will answer; and while they are yet speaking, I will hear. The wolf and the lamb shall feed together, and the lion shall eat straw like the bullock: and dust *shall* be the serpent's meat. They shall not hurt nor destroy in all my holy mountain, saith the Lord."

What a day of rejoicing it will be for the followers of the true God! All who've come into the millennium are going to enjoy the fruit and works of their hands, because His will be a perfect economic system, with prosperity for all.

Right now, millions of Americans—Christians included—are living on tranquilizers because of the pressures of life, and because there seems to be no way out of their despair. But during the millennium period believers will not need valium, pills, or other artificial stimulants to keep them going. Why? Because the redeemed who will enter the millennial kingdom will be changed, and energized by the power of Jesus Christ. Something wonderful will even begin to happen in the animal world. A calmness will come over groups of animals that were once enemies. There will be no more need for cages, zoos, or restricted areas in the wild animal parks throughout the world.

Isaiah 11:6–9 says, "The wolf also shall dwell with the lamb, and the leopard shall lie down with the kid; and the calf and the young lion and the fatling together; and a little child shall lead them. And the cow and the bear shall feed; their young ones shall lie down together: and the lion shall eat straw like the ox. And the sucking child shall play on the hole of the asp, and the weaned child shall put his hand on the cockatrice's den. They shall not hurt nor destroy in all my holy mountain: for the earth shall be full of the knowledge of the Lord, as the waters cover the sea."

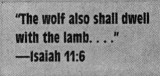

"The wolf also shall dwell with the lamb. . . ."
—Isaiah 11:6

What a day that will be! We will not even need the light of the sun, for Revelation 21:23 states: "And the city had no need of the sun, neither of the moon, to shine in it; for the glory of God did lighten it and the Lamb is the light thereof."

It even gets better. Isaiah 65:20 promises, "There shall be no more thence an infant of days, nor an old man that hath not filled his days: for the child shall die an hundred years old; but the sinner *being* an hundred years old shall be accursed."

## FINALLY, THE FOUNTAIN OF YOUTH

IMAGINE. A child will be considered youthful at one hundred years. Do you remember the Spanish explorer Juan Ponce de Leon (c. 1460–1521)? As a teenager he joined the Spanish forces that eventually defeated the Moors of Granada, and in 1493 he joined Christopher Columbus on his second voyage to America. Ponce de Leon helped crush Indian revolts on the island of Hispaniola and was rewarded in 1508 with a commission to explore Borinquen (Puerto Rico). He was an amazing man, with so many military accomplishments.

But what was he really after? According to legend, he was seeking the Fountain of Youth—a rejuvenating, tonic spring that the people of the Caribbean had so often described. However, de Leon was mortally wounded by an Indian arrow and returned to Havana, where he died, never having found the Fountain of Youth for which he had searched so long. But we who are redeemed will find it, know it, will drink from it, and be refreshed by it—forever. The best part of this entire scenario is that those who believe will be eternally in the presence of God, beholding our Lord's beauty forever and forever.

## EVERLASTING LIFE WITH THE KING OF KINGS

UNTIL THEN, we will have to "go through it to get to it." However, the "getting through" phase of the journey is accelerating as never before. We are literally on the edge of eternity. We are now on the other side of time. Prophecies are being fulfilled as in no other era of history. It is my fervent hope that you have a personal relationship with this Savior of mankind, and that you will be present with Him in His new kingdom forever. Because it's all about to happen. The King will soon come, and those who know Him will enjoy everlasting life with Him.

For the first nine chapters of this book we've looked at the signs of His coming. We've reviewed passage after passage of Scripture that have prophesied the coming of the end times and the triumphant return of Jesus Christ.

Now, as we come to the final pages of this book, I want to close with a literal "Hallelujah Chorus" of joy and praise. Why? Because we eagerly await our entrance into the presence of the Lord of Hosts, the Lord of Righteousness, the Most High, the Rod of Jesse, the Lawgiver, the Messiah, the Prince, and the Sun of Righteousness, for His glorious reign.

## THE RAPTURE, THE REVELATION, AND PROPHETICAL SIGNS

CHRIST'S RETURN IS DESCRIBED as the "blessed hope" in Titus 2:13: "Looking for that blessed hope, and the glorious appearing of the great God and our Savior Jesus Christ."

The happiness of the greatest event in world history has to do with seeing Jesus. If this thought does not bring joy and peace to one's heart, something is drastically wrong. The great hymn often sung by believers should be the position of every child of God. This song declares:

> "Friends will be there I have loved long ago;
> joy like a river around me will flow.
> Yet just a smile from my Saviour I know,
> will through the ages be glory for me."

Amen.

### THE RAPTURE

MULTITUDES TODAY are unaware that there are two stages or phases within the process of the Second Coming—the Rapture and the Revelation—and that these events are separated by a seven-year period of time. From what I have studied over the years, I believe the Rapture is the next occurrence on God's calendar. This Rapture is the literal, visible, and bodily return of Christ in the heavens. Acts 1:9–11 states: "And when he had spoken these things, while they beheld, he was taken up; and a cloud received him out of their sight. And while they looked steadfastly toward heaven as he went up, behold, two men stood by them in white apparel; Which also said, Ye men of Galilee, why stand ye gazing up into heaven? this same Jesus, which is taken up from you into heaven, shall so come in like manner as ye have seen him go into heaven."

Has Christ already returned? Some cultists declare that He came in 1914 or 1918 as an invisible spirit. Nothing could be further from the truth! The Bible declares that He shall return as He left. A person can easily know how He left by studying Luke 24:39. Christ, in His new, resurrected body, said, "Behold my hands and my feet, that it is I myself: handle me, and see; for a spirit hath not flesh and bones, as ye see me have."

He adds in verse 41, "Have ye here any meat?" As you may recall, the disciples then gave Christ a piece of broiled fish and honeycomb which He took and ate while they were watching (verses 42, 43). The risen Savior had a body of flesh and bones—a body that could be seen, touched, and fed. This same Christ, in the same body, shall come "in like manner" from heaven. When He returns in the heavens, all believers—dead and living—will also be taken bodily to meet Him in the clouds. One day soon, the people of God are going to disappear from the earth in a blaze of glory.

## THE STAGE IS SET FOR THE RAPTURE OF THE CHURCH

AS A NEW CHRISTIAN, I painted a message on the glove compartment of my automobile. It said, "The driver of this car is awaiting the return of Christ. At His coming, Christians will disappear bodily from the earth. Should I suddenly vanish, take over the steering wheel."

I can still remember the looks on the faces of hitch-hikers as they read my startling message. Many of them declared, "Buddy, the next corner is as far as I go!" It was true then, and it's true today: those who do not have a relationship with the King of kings have great difficulty accepting the glorious teaching of the Rapture. The Christian, on the other hand, accepts by faith the declarations of the Word of God concerning this subject which is becoming increasingly important with every passing day.

First Thessalonians 4:16–18 states, "For the Lord Himself shall descend from heaven with a shout, with the voice of the archangel and with the trump of God: and the dead in Christ shall rise first: then we which are alive *and* remain shall be caught up together with them in the clouds, to meet the Lord in the air, and so shall we ever be with the Lord."

Verse 14 declares that when Christ comes at the time of the Rapture, He will bring those who sleep (the dead) with Him. At this point, you may be saying, "Finally! I've found my first contradiction in the Bible! How can Christ *bring the dead* with Him (verse 14) and also *come after the dead* (verse 16)?" There are no contradictions in the Word of God. On the contrary, it is the finite, limited intellect of human beings that cannot grasp the infinite, unlimited mind of the omniscient God. And if one is led by the Holy Spirit, and takes the time to study under His direction, so-called contradictions will immediately fade into obscurity.

Can Christ *bring the dead* with Him in verse 14 and *come after the dead* in verse 16? Here is the solution: When a believer dies, his spirit and soul go into the presence of God, but his body goes into the grave. To be absent from the body is to be present with the Lord (see 2 Corinthians 5:8). This soul, absent from the body, is with Christ until the great day when body, soul, and spirit are reunited at the coming of Jesus.

Then, Christ brings the dead (soul and spirit) with Him—in verse 14—to come after the dead (the body)—in verse 16. When the "dead rise first," it is the body—only the body—that comes out of the grave to be reunited with the soul and spirit brought to the body from heaven. This does away with the unscriptural teaching of "soul sleep."

The next point is of extreme importance. If the Lord comes to receive the bodies of the dead in Christ, will He leave the bodies of the living in Christ behind? If this were so, the wisest thing to do at the sound of the trumpet would be to commit suicide. This, however, is not the case, for the Bible declares, "the dead in Christ shall rise first: then, we which are alive and remain shall be caught up together with them [the dead] in the clouds, to meet the Lord in the air: and so shall we ever be with the Lord." Thus, we see that the Rapture is a bodily resurrection for the dead and living who are in Christ, or who are born again.

The entire occurrence is going to take place in half a blink: "Behold, I shew you a mystery; We shall not all sleep [be dead], but we shall all be changed, in a moment, In the twinkling of an eye, at the last trump: for the trumpet shall sound, and the dead shall be raised incorruptible, and we shall be changed. For this corruptible [the dead] must put on incorruption, and this mortal [the living] must put on immortality" (1 Corinthians 15:51–53).

> One scientific company has calculated the twinkling of an eye to be approximately eleven one hundredths of a second.

One scientific company has calculated the twinkling of an eye to be approximately eleven one hundredths of a second. In this moment of time, we take upon ourselves immortality and are transformed to be like Jesus. First John 3:2 reports that when [we see Jesus] "we shall be like him; for we shall see him as he is."

Again, Philippians 3:20–21 verifies that our bodies will be changed as we enter into God's presence in whirlwind style.

These verses tell us that "our citizenship is in heaven, from whence also we look for the Savior. . . . who shall change our vile bodies, that they may be fashioned like unto his glorious body."

There are those who may say, "I don't believe in the Rapture, because the word cannot be found in the Bible." The word "Bible" cannot be found in the Bible, either, but this does not disprove the Bible's existence. Terms are coined to portray the experiences they picture, and the word *rapture* comes from the Latin word *rapio,* which means "a snatching away." The passages above offer proof enough that the Bible teaches us that there shall be a snatching away. Since *rapio* translated from Latin to English means "a snatching away," only the willfully ignorant will reject such a clear-cut term to describe the first phase of the second coming of Christ.

## THE REVELATION

THE SECOND PHASE of the Second Coming, described as "the Revelation" will take place seven years after the Rapture. Again, the term *revelation* is a coined word, picturing the truth it depicts. *Revelation* comes from the word *revealing.* When Christ returns to earth, He will reveal Himself to all the inhabitants of the globe. Hence, this event is called "the Revelation," or "revealing of Christ."

Scripturally, Revelation 4:1 describes phase one of the return of Christ, while Revelation 19:11 depicts phase two. Fix these two chapters firmly in your mind, and prophecy will become a stabilized blessing in your life. The "come up hither" of Revelation 4:1 is the Rapture—the meeting in the air. The appearance of the white horse rider and His armies in Revelation 19:11 is the Revelation of Jesus Christ.

Chapter 4 removes the believer from the judgments described in chapters 6–18; chapter 19 restores him to his earthly sojourn after the judgments are completed. Chapter 4, depicting the Rapture, occurs before the seven years of tribulation described in chapters 6–18; chapter 19 describes the return of the King and His people, after the horrendous catastrophes of chapters 6–18 have transpired. We know this to be true because the Book of Revelation is written chronologically, with the tribulation hour taking place in chapters 6–18. The Church is removed in chapter 4, and the tribulation follows in chapters 6–18. Then the saints return at the conclusion of the tribulation hour in chapter 19.

> When Christ returns to earth, He will reveal Himself to all the inhabitants of the globe.

In addition, Revelation 3:10 states, "Because thou hast kept the word of my patience, I also will keep thee from [not through (preservation) but from (the Greek—*ek*—out of)] the hour of temptation, which shall come upon all the world, to try them that dwell upon the earth." This will be the world's most terrifying hour. All the wars of the past will look like Sunday school picnics in comparison.

Jeremiah 30:7 says, "Alas! for that day is great, [there is none] like it."

Daniel 12:1—"There shall be a time of trouble, such as never was since there was a nation *even* to that same time."

Joel 2:1, 2—"Let all the inhabitants of the land tremble: for the day of the Lord cometh, for it is *nigh* at hand; a day of darkness and of gloominess, a day of clouds and thick darkness. . . . there hath [never] been . . . the like."

Jesus said in Matthew 24:21, "For then shall be great tribulation, such as [never was] since the beginning of the world to this time, no, nor ever shall be."

When it occurs, fiery incineration will engulf the globe:

- "The Lord will come with fire" (Isaiah 66:15).

- "The flaming flame shall not be quenched" (Ezekiel 20:47).

- "A fire [devours] before them" (Joel 2:3).

- "The whole land shall be devoured by the fire of his jealousy" (Zephaniah 1:18).

- "Their flesh shall consume away while they stand upon their feet, and their eyes shall consume away in their holes, and their tongue shall consume away in their mouth" (Zechariah 14:12).

- "The third part of trees was burnt up, and all green grass was burnt up" (Revelation 8:7).

- "By these three was the third part of men killed, by the fire, and by the smoke, and by the brimstone" (Revelation 9:18).

The fire of the tribulation hour lies just ahead for the human race. The saved will be removed before it begins. They are described as "taken" in Revelation 4:1, and they experience the judgment seat of Christ before the chapter ends. In fact, we find them placing crowns (their rewards) at the feet of the Savior in verses 10 and 11. And remember, no one is rewarded until the resurrection of the just occurs (Luke 14:14). This is proof that the saved are safe and secure when the judgments begin in chapter 6. Then, when the blitzkrieg ends in chapter 18, the saved return with Christ as He appears to the inhabitants of the earth and becomes their King.

Revelation 19:11–16 gives us a glimpse of the momentous event:

"And I saw heaven opened; and behold a white horse; and he that sat upon him *was* called Faithful and True, and in righteousness he doth judge and make war. His eyes *were* as a flame of fire, and on his head were many crowns; and he had a name written, that no man knew, but he himself. And he was clothed with a vesture dipped in blood: and his name is called The Word of God. And the armies *which where* in heaven followed him upon white horses, clothed in fine linen, white and clean.

And out of his mouth goeth a sharp sword, that with it he should smite the nations: and he shall rule them with a rod of iron: and he treadeth the winepress of the fierceness and wrath of almighty God. And he hath on his thigh a name written, KING OF KINGS, AND LORD OF LORDS."

This is the revealing of Christ to the nations. At His revelation, every eye will see His glory. "Behold he cometh with clouds; and every eye shall see him" (Revelation 1:7).

The armies following Him from heaven to earth are the saints who were removed from earth in Revelation 4:1.They were evacuated before the great holocaust began. They are the same crowd mentioned in Jude, verse 14: "Behold, the Lord cometh with ten thousands of His saints." The Hebrews and Greeks had no terminology to describe millions, billions, trillions, or quadrillions. They simply said, "ten thousands." Thus, the innumerable company of saints following the Lord to earth are the redeemed.

## THE SIGNIFICANCE OF PROPHETICAL SIGNS

WHAT RELATIONSHIP exists between the Rapture, the Revelation, and prophetical signs? Where do they fit into the schedule of events described in God's Word? Many think the signs point to phase one, the Rapture, because they identify the snatching away as the Second Coming of Christ in their minds. Doctrinally speaking, this is not so. The actual Second Coming of Christ is the second phase—the Revelation, or the revealing of Christ to the inhabitants of earth. Since He came to earth at His first advent, He must come to earth at His second advent. The Rapture is not Christ's appearance upon earth, but a meeting in the heavens—an intermediary evacuation of believers from earth before the storm. Seven years later, Christ will come to earth, touching down on the Mount of Olives (see Zechariah 14:4).

The prophetical signs, then, point to Christ's return to earth with His saints at the close of the tribulation hour—not to the Rapture. Here's how that statement can be proved. Take two Bibles and place them side by side. Open one to Revelation 6 where the signs begin to be fulfilled. Open the other to Matthew 24, Mark 13, and Luke 17 or 21, where Christ's prophetical predictions are recorded. The inescapable conclusion is that the signs are identical!

> **What relationship exists between the Rapture, the Revelation, and prophetical signs?**

Here's the significance of this. The Church is taken in Revelation 4, and the signs take place two chapters later. The signs of Revelation 6 are identical to the predictions of Christ in the four Gospels, proving that the signs Jesus gave point to His revelation, the second phase of the Second Coming. Even if there were not a sign yet in existence, believers could be called home any moment. This is true because each of the signs could occur during the seven-year period following the believers' departure. Remember, the signs point to Christ's Second Coming to earth (Revelation 19).

Now, the reason I believe we may go home any moment is that Jesus said, "When ye shall see all these things [signs—not one, not two, but *all the signs* occurring simultaneously, then] know that it is near, even at the door" (Matthew 24:33). What is near when a person sees all the signs occurring? Christ's return to earth—the Revelation, phase two.

When this event takes place, we Christians will return with Him. All the signs pointing to the return of Christ with His saints—the return of the King with His armies—are already in their beginning stages. The signs indicate we are coming back with the Lord soon. How can this be, as long as we are still present on earth? There is but one logical conclusion. We must be removed very soon via phase one, the Rapture, in order to return with Christ, via phase two, the Revelation. Jesus Himself had much to say about His revelation. And I hope that you, too, are moving further down the road toward understanding your own earthly and heavenly future, and the astonishing prophecies predicting His spectacular return.

## THE MILLENNIUM—A SUBJECT OF GREAT CONFUSION

THE SUBJECT of the millennium seems to be one of the most misunderstood, confusing portions of Scripture for many Christians. For instance, many believe that Russia must march at the inception of the seven-year tribulation period and be defeated within the first few weeks of the conflict. In their minds, this is imperative so that the "burning of weapons for seven years" (Ezekiel 39:9) is completed before a perfect world under Messiah is established.

In reading the works of more than 130 authors from every theological position imaginable on this subject, I have concluded that the teaching of the thousand-year reign of Christ has often been mythicized and erroneously taught. That's why in these last pages I want to address a few of these confusing, often misinterpreted theories.

In times like these, it's difficult to imagine a future age when the earth will be restored, when disease will be eliminated, when there will be no pornography on the newsstands (or the Internet,) no drunkenness, no drug addiction, and when lives will be so lengthened that a hundred-year-old shall be thought of as a mere child. But, my friends, we are that close to such an age—the literal thousand-year reign of Jesus Christ on earth.

We who know Christ often focus much attention on the tribulation events leading up to the return of Jesus to earth. In doing so, we tend to overlook or misunderstand the many volumes of biblical references detailing what will be the most exciting, glorious, and fulfilling time in the history of man—the period known as the millennium.

"But Dr. Van Impe," you might say, "the millennium is not for today's believers. We'll be raptured out of the world before the tribulation. The millennial age is only for those people who survive Armageddon and for their offspring." I must politely disagree, because I see nothing in Scripture to support that theological point of view. Those of us who are taken out of this world—never to experience death—will, in a unique way, witness and very much be a part of the millennial age. What do I mean?

## A City "Hanging" in Space

JUDE 14 teaches that we believers will return with Christ. We will be living in a city hovering above the earthly city of Jerusalem and watching and interacting with the world below. That's right. This is precisely what the Bible says. I know it sounds strange—a city, the New Jerusalem, just hanging out there in space. As a teenager, I first read about this in Revelation 21:2, 21:9 and 22:5. I thought, *That can't be. A city hanging in space? Who could even imagine such a thing?* Then, in 1969, our astronauts landed on the moon. From that vantage point the astronauts looked at the earth and discovered that it, like the moon they walked on, was also hanging in space.

In effect, the earth itself, spinning at 25,000 miles per day, is a world suspended in space and upheld by the power of the Lord Jesus Christ, exactly as we read in Hebrews 1:3. Since the concept of a spatial city is both rational and intelligible, especially in light of today's space travel and the establishment of space stations, it is not so hard to imagine the impending advent of this Holy City.

So, in effect, the earth itself—spinning at 25,000 miles per day—is a world suspended in space and upheld by the power of God.

This "New Jerusalem"—a city so bright that its glow lights the world both day and night—is where we will be living in new spiritual bodies. Those bodies will allow us to walk through walls, disappear and reappear

> . . . The earth . . . is a world suspended in space and upheld by the power of God.

at will, and travel at the speed of our own desires, just as Jesus did in His resurrection body (see Acts 1:9–11).

Do you remember how the disciples recognized the Lord after He rose from the grave? Do you recall how they could touch Him and feel His flesh and bones? And how Jesus went out and did some fishing, prepared a meal for His followers, and ate with them? Jesus was seen in this resurrection body by between five hundred and a thousand people, according to biblical accounts (1 Corinthians 1 5:3–8).

## GLORIFIED BODIES

THE WORD OF GOD says we're going to be like Jesus after the Rapture. According to 1 Thessalonians 4:16–17, the dead in Christ shall rise first. Then, we're told in 1 Corinthians 15:51, in the twinkling of an eye, we who are alive on earth at the appointed hour shall be caught up together with the dead in the clouds to meet the Lord in the air.

As we sweep through the heavenlies to meet Him, we're changed to be like Jesus. We'll receive our new glorified bodies—flesh and bones but apparently minus the blood. We won't need blood to remove the impurities of our bodies at that time. "The life of the flesh is in the blood, but not the life of the spirit" (Leviticus 17:11).

The psalmist says in Psalm 17:15: "I shall be satisfied, when I awake, with thy likeness." When Jesus comes He will change our vile bodies, not leave them behind. Philippians 3:21 says they will be fashioned like unto His glorious body. And 1 John 3:2 adds: "When we see Jesus, we shall be like him."

Like Jesus, in spirit-bodies we will be able to be seen, to be touched, to partake of food, and to co-mingle with the people of the earth. That is the message of Luke 24:39–42. Imagine! We will be able to move across the universe at the speed of our own thoughts. And we will be living in that new holy city that hovers over the globe in the millennial era.

Meanwhile, there will be people down below—on earth—living in their old human bodies under the rule of Jesus. It will be a very different world from the one we know today. There will be justice. Death will be known, but life will be greatly extended—especially for those who avoid sin. Although Satan will be bound in chains during this period, the world will not be without temptation as the people of this time will still be partakers of an old sinful nature. This is why their children rebel at the conclusion of the millennium (Revelation 20:8, 9).

Sin will be greatly reduced, but it will still be a part of this new world. And sin will determine how brief or how long people live. How is sin possible if Satan is bound and Christ rules the world with a rod of iron? James expounds this theory clearly in chapter 1, verses 13–15:

> "Let no man say when he is tempted, I am tempted of God: for God cannot be tempted with evil, neither tempteth he any man; But every man is tempted, when he is driven away of his own lust, and enticed. Then when lust hath conceived, it bringeth forth sin: and sin, when it is finished, bringeth forth death."

### CLEARING UP THE CONFUSION

UNFORTUNATELY, MANY Christians misunderstand this millennial era. They usually think that once Christ comes back as King, and the world is a new creation, then everything will be perfect. This is simply not so. After the thousand-year period when the new heavens and new earth are created, as depicted in Revelation 2 1:1, then there will be perfection. But during this millennial age, Jesus begins the process of regenerating the earth. He gives it new life.

Acts 3:19 refers to this period as a time of refreshing.

Acts 3:21 calls it a time of restitution (or restoration).

Matthew 19:28 calls it the regeneration.

After World War II, it took years to rebuild Germany and Japan. It's going to take even longer to repair the damage that man has wrought on the earth during the seven-year period of tribulation. For instance, consider Revelation 6:3–8:

- The rider on the red horse removes peace from the earth and the globe is engulfed in mass war.

- The rider on the black horse creates worldwide famine.

- The rider on the pale horse spreads pestilences.

In Revelation 8:7, a third of all the trees in the world are consumed by fire. In Revelation 9:18, one of every three men on the planet is killed by fire, smoke, and brimstone.

In Revelation 16:3, every living soul, or creature, in the sea is destroyed. In Revelation 16:21, a great earthquake strikes, more destructive than any man has ever witnessed.

Do you get the picture?

## CHRIST APPEARS WHEN EARTH IS AT ITS WORST

THIS WORLD is going to be a mess when Jesus returns. It's going to be a pile of rubble. It's simply not theologically accurate to say that Jesus will return only after we prepare and restore the world for Him. Christ comes when things are at their worst, and He comes personally to supervise the restoration of the world during this period of a thousand years. Jesus not only restores the earth during this time, but He also enforces a thousand-year armistice. It will be a time when war will be unknown. There will be no soldiers in uniform, no armament plans, no military camps. Hospitals will be shut down, for there will be little need of doctors and nurses. There will be no poverty, violence, or crime. There will be no wastelands, no storms, no droughts, no crop failures, no floods. As we mentioned in chapter 9, even the wild animals will be tame and harmless and will stop devouring each other (Isaiah 11:6). Globally, it will be a time of perfect peace until the final days of the thousand-year period. Then Satan is released and war against Christ occurs (Revelation 20:8, 9).

In this glorious period, vice will be unknown because Christ won't allow it. There will be a "zero tolerance" attitude toward evil. In Revelation 19:15, we're told that the Lord will rule the world with a rod of iron. That's the difference. Jesus will be here as a benevolent dictator. The world will be operating under a true theocracy. Today, we think of a theocracy as a government ruled by a church or religious figure. But the root word, *theos*, means "God." So the millennium will truly see the world ruled by God Himself.

If you ask me where we find such startling information, there is but one answer—the Bible—the living Word of God. It's full of wonderful accounts of that coming age of full redemption and creation's restoration.

## THE BREAKING OF "STUBBORN NATURES"

JESUS INSTRUCTED us to pray, "Thy Kingdom come, Thy will be done, on earth as it is in heaven" (Matthew 6:10; Luke 11:2). While we won't experience complete righteousness until after the millennial kingdom, this period will literally see tne Lord's will done on earth as it is in heaven. But there will be times Christ will have to break stubborn, carnal wills (Psalm 2:9). The people on earth at this time will be much like people today—they will bear children who have the Adamic nature (Romans 5:12), and by the end of the millennial age, some of these children will become rebellious. When Satan is unleashed once again before the final judgment, multitudes of these rebels will actually join forces with the devil.

> Jesus instructed us to pray, "Thy kindgom come, Thy will be done. . . ."

During the millennium, people will remain under control for one reason—because Jesus will break their stubborn natures with that "rod of iron." The wickedness of the human heart is incorrigible. Even without the presence of Satan, people will go astray. All of humanity will enter the millennium righteous and repentant. But they will bear children who turn away from God—even though they can see Him and have direct access to Him.

If the Lord can't convince people after a thousand years, it's amazing that we can ever effectively preach the gospel and win souls in our world today. Only by the grace and mercy of God and the conviction of the Holy Spirit do people come to experience salvation. As long as people are confined by their human natures, there will always be mockers and scoffers—people who doubt God even when they can see Him living in and ruling their own world.

Yet, today, even among believers, there are those who doubt the reality of the coming millennium. To disbelieve that Jesus will reign on earth for a thousand years is to cast a long shadow of disbelief on the Bible itself. There are literally hundreds of verses backing up what I say about this period. Here are just a handful of such references with which to begin your own personal study:

- Psalm 2:6—"I will set my king upon my holy hill of Zion."

- Zechariah 14:2-4—"For I will gather all nations against Jerusalem to battle; and the city shall be taken, and the houses rifled, and the women ravished; and half of the city shall go forth into captivity, and the residue of the people shall not be cut off from the city. Then shall the Lord go forth, and fight against those nations, as when he fought in the day of battle.

  "And his feet shall stand in that day upon the mount of Olives, which *is* before Jerusalem on the east, and the mount of Olives shall cleave in the midst thereof toward the east and toward the west, *and there shall be* a very great valley; and half of the mountain shall remove toward the north, and half of it toward the south." Then judgment falls on the invaders. Zechariah 14:12–16: "And this shall be the plague wherewith the LORD will smite all the people that have fought against Jerusalem. Their flesh shall consume away while they stand upon their feet, and their eyes shall consume away in their holes, and their tongue shall consume away in their mouth. And it shall come to pass in *that* day that a great tumult from the LORD shall be among them; and they shall lay hold every one on the hand of his neighbour, and his hand shall rise up against the hand of his neighbour. And Judah also shall fight at Jerusalem; and the wealth of all the heathen round about shall be gathered together, gold, and silver, and apparel, in great abundance. And so shall be the plague of the horse, of the mule, of the camel, and of the ass, and of all the beasts that shall be in these tents, as this plague. And it shall come to pass, *that* every one that is left of all the nations which came against Jerusalem shall even go up from year to year to worship the King, the LORD of hosts, and to keep the feast of tabernacles.

- Revelation 19:11–15—Christ enters the world with His armies. In verse 15, it states that He will rule the nations with a rod of iron.

- Revelation 20:4–6—Christ is depicted setting up His millennial kingdom. Verse 6 once again refers to Jesus reigning a thousand years.

To discount such profound, detailed prophecy borders on heresy. Both the Old and New Testaments refer clearly and frequently to this period in history—to Christ's return and His thousand-year reign. Multitudes of rabbis who lived two centuries before Christ was born also mentioned a thousand-year period of tranquility upon earth, and immense documentation backs this truth.

## SETTING THE RECORD STRAIGHT

THOSE WHO BELIEVE that no millennium will ever occur are called *amillennialists,* meaning "without a millennium." Those called *postmillennialists* theorize that we must herald in Christ's return and the kingdom age by first cleaning up man's act. *Premillennialists* believe the Church will be raptured prior to the tribulation, and the saints will return with Him for His thousand-year reign.

Amillennialists are forced to ignore countless passages in the Bible to make their case; postmillennialists must read things into Scripture that suggest Christ reenters a placid and tranquil world. Nowhere does Scripture describe either scenario. It's not going to get better before Jesus comes; it will become worse, as we learn in 2 Timothy 3:13, which is further confirmed by what we have learned in the first nine chapters of this book.

I have no desire to create unnecessary division among Christian brothers and sisters, or to cast aspersions against other believers. But I must declare as firmly and as forthrightly as I can that the premillennial view is the doctrine reflected in God's Word. It is vanity to suggest God needs man to usher in His kingdom. God is sovereign. He keeps His promises. As promised, Jesus is going to come again and rule the world in His own way. And the time is at hand.

**God is sovereign. He keeps His promises.**

In the days of Noah, God's command was "come in"; in Lot's day, it was "come out"; in our day, it will be "come up!" It has been a fact of history that God always spares His own from judgment. When the horrendous worldwide flood came in Noah's day, Noah told those who were prepared to *come in* to the ark (Genesis 7:7). When judgment fell on the wickedness of Sodom and Gomorrah in Genesis 19:14, the angels told Lot and his family to *come out* of the city if they were to be rescued. In our day, we will be invited to *come up,* as we live out the prophecy of Revelation 4:1 which says, "After this I looked, and, behold, a door was opened in heaven: and the first voice which I heard *was* as it were of a trumpet talking with me; which said, Come up hither, and I will shew thee things which must be hereafter."

## HOPE FOR ALL

DURING THE TRIBULATION that follows the Rapture, all hell is going to break loose on planet earth. It will be a furious time because the hindering power of the Holy Spirit will be temporarily removed from earth. That's believers (1 Corinthians 3:16; 6:19). How bad will things get? Revelation 9:18 indicates that a third of mankind will be killed by fire, smoke, and brimstone. That is nothing less than a first-century way of explaining all-out thermonuclear warfare. Imagine. But as terrible as that fate sounds, there is still hope for those left behind. As long as one is alive, there is hope. Joel chapter 2 and Acts chapter 2 describe the calamitous tribulation period. The good news is that in the middle of the carnage and destruction, Joel 2:32 and Acts 2:21 give us the hope that "whosoever shall call upon the name of the Lord shall be saved."

There is always hope in Jesus—then, and now. We as Christians should not be fearful and despondent, "sitting out" the next few years while history unfolds, remaining uninvolved in the affairs of our world because we "know the ending of the Book." We should not carry an attitude of despair and foreboding into our churches, our work places, and our family lives. Instead, as believers, we have cause for rejoicing in the truth: Christ is coming again to earth as He promised

He would. And because He promises to come "as a thief in the night," we must expect His return at any moment.

It may be today. It may be tomorrow. But one thing is certain. Christ is coming soon. We are biblically mandated to occupy until He comes. That does not mean to sit down—as in to occupy a chair. It means, instead, to work, to understand the meaning of His return, and to continue to share the Good News with those who do not know our Savior today and every day.

Yes, it's late. Very late. The clock has almost struck midnight, and yet there are multitudes who have not yet invited Jesus Christ into their lives. The final hour has not yet come, but it is fast approaching. Be ready for the world-shattering events of the year 2001 and beyond as we find ourselves teetering on the edge of eternity.

## An Invitation and a Warning

THIS FINAL CHAPTER closes with an invitation and a warning. The invitation is to come to Jesus, and to accept Him as Savior and Lord. The warning is that no one must ever manipulate, add to, or take away any of God's inspired word of prophecy. That's why the amazing passage in Revelation 22:17–21 is the real conclusion—not just to this book, made by man, but to the Book of books, inspired by God the Father, our King of kings, and Lord of lords:

> "And the Spirit and the bride say, Come. And let him that heareth say, Come. And let him that is athirst come. And whosoever will, let him take the water of life freely. For I testify unto every man that heareth the words of the prophecy of this book, If any man shall add unto these things, God shall add unto him the plagues that are written in this book: And if any man shall take away from the words of the book of this prophecy, God shall take away his part out of the book of life, and out of the holy city, and from the things which are written in this book. He

which testifieth these things saith, Surely I come quickly. Amen. Even so, come, Lord Jesus. The grace of our Lord Jesus Christ *be* with you all. Amen."

## AFTERWORD

As we've seen, *millennium*, which means "one thousand years," refers to the kingdom of Christ on earth. This era, foretold by all the prophets, will be a time of peace among people and nations. War will be but a relic of the past. Jerusalem, known for war, bloodshed, and international tensions, will at last become the city of peace and the capitol of the world. The Prince of Peace will rule from David's throne and the promises given to Mary concerning Jesus will be fulfilled (Luke 1:32, 33; Isaiah 9:6, 7).

Peace will finally come to Israel and to the world. The Prince of Peace will once and for all come, bringing His lasting peace. When the governments of earth have finally fallen, the Messiah of Israel—the Saviour of men—will set up His kingdom (Daniel 2:44), and Satan will be bound for one thousand years (Revelation 20:1–3).

There will be persons with mortal bodies and persons with glorified bodies on earth during this time. Those who survived the tribulation, who have not been condemned in the judgment of the nations (Matthew 25:3–46), will be allowed to enter the millennium in their mortal bodies. They will have prolonged lives. Along with the millions of babies born during this time, these persons will live for the entire one thousand years of Christ's reign. If, at the end of this era, they have not rebelled with Satan and have chosen to accept Jesus as their Saviour and Lord, they will live on eternally.

Their immortal lives will not be spent in glorified bodies but in human bodies eternally preserved through partaking of the tree of life. Some theologians believe they receive glorified bodies at the conclusion of the millennium. We'll wait and see.

> "It is my prayer that you will be ready to meet our Savior and Lord as He comes to take His children home."
> —Dr. Jack Van Impe

They will retain perfect health and will not experience aging because of the leaves of the trees that grow for the healing of the nations (Revelation 22:2). The millennium will also bring peace in the world of nature. All of God's creation suffered as a result of the fall of man and will be restored at this time (Romans 8:20–23). Nature will cooperate with man again (Genesis 3:17, 18); productivity will return (Zechariah 8:12), earthquakes, tornadoes, floods, and the other calamities we are experiencing with such violence today—and will only see accelerate in our lifetimes—will be no more. Even the animal world will be at peace with man and with each other (Isaiah 11:6–8).

All economic conflict will be swept away. Oppression and strikes will be unknown, and there will be an abundance of food and housing for all (Isaiah 65:21–23). There will be religious peace with Jews and Gentiles, worshipping the Lord together (Isaiah 11:9, 10) as the Jews will finally be at peace in their own land (Ezekiel 36:24–27). All this will happen because the Kingdom Age (millennium) will be characterized by the fullness of the Spirit (Joel 2:28, 29) more than in any previous epoch of history.

However, no person who has turned his back on the Savior in willful disbelief will enter the millennium (the Jews as a nation will have recognized and accepted Christ as Messiah during the tribulation [Romans 11:26] and the Gentiles will have experienced conversion prior to admission also). Earth's motto will finally be "Holiness unto the Lord" (Zechariah 14:20, 21).

Those reigning with Christ during this time are the returning saints (the Church, the Bride of Christ—Jude 14; Revelation 19:14), the resurrected Old Testament saints (Daniel 12:2), and the raised tribulation saints (Revelation 20:4). Each group, brought to faith in Christ during different dispensations of time, has different duties to perform. The Church is the Bride of Christ and enjoys the one-thousand-year honeymoon upon earth while reigning with Him.

Such is the picture of earth's future. We are not there yet, but the day of His appearing is quickly approaching. It is my prayer that you will be ready to meet our Savior and Lord as He comes to take His children home.

"Surely I come quickly. Amen. Even so, come, Lord Jesus. The grace of our Lord Jesus Christ be with you all. Amen" (Revelation 22:21). The final blessed benediction of God's Holy Book!

## Also by Dr. Jack Van Impe

*Revelation Revealed*

*Israel's Final Holocaust*

*Everything You Always Wanted to Know About Prophecy*

*Your Future: An A-Z Index to Prophecy*

*Unmasking and Triumphing Over the Spirit of Antichrist*

*11:59 and Counting!!*

*The Judgment Seat of Christ*

*Religious Reprobates and Saved Sinners*

*The True Gospel*

*This is Christianity*

*The Cost of Discipleship*

*Exorcism and the Spirit World*

*Sabotaging the World Church*

*Alcohol: The Beloved Enemy*

*Sin's Explosion*

Dr. Jack Van Impe has preached the gospel face-to-face to more people than any evangelist except Dr. Billy Graham. More than one million souls have been saved through Jack Van Impe Ministries. He and his wife Rexella have delivered the gospel message to audiences totaling ten million in city-wide crusades across America and Canada. Today, the couple co-anchors *Jack Van Impe Presents,* a news-style television and radio program examining current headlines in the light of Bible prophecy. *Jack Van Impe Presents* is carried in 25,000 cities in North America, and reaches 160 nations around the globe. The Van Impes have received nineteen Angel Awards for excellence in media presentation. Dr. Van Impe has written twenty-five books and produced twenty videocassettes with a combined distribution of 1.25 million copies. As a leading Christian apologist and promoter of unity within the Body of Christ, Dr. Van Impe has appeared on two hundred talk shows and has been featured in articles in *U.S. News & World Report,* *Time,* and *Newsweek,* as well as in scores of newspapers. He has been honored by thirteen leading colleges and seminaries with doctoral degrees in the field of theology, and has committed over fourteen thousand verses of Scripture to memory.